The BARBECUE Cookbook

A tasty Heidelberg Dinner (see page 35).
Baked Trout (see page 46).

First published by Summit Books
176 South Creek Road, Dee Why West, N.S.W. 2099, Australia
© Copyright RPLA Pty Limited 1981
Produced in Australia by the Publisher
Typeset in Australia by Savage and Co. Pty Ltd
Typeset in Cairo 11pt solid
Printed by Kyoda-Shing Loong Printing Industries Pte Ltd
112 Neythal Road, Jurong Town, Singapore 22

Published in this edition by Galley Press,
an imprint of W H Smith and Son Limited
Registered No 237811 England.

Trading as WHS Distributors, St John's
House, East Street, Leicester, LEI 6NE

ISBN 0 86136 910 6

The
BARBECUE
Cookbook

Galley Press

Acknowledgements

Food preparation and photographs styled by Ann Fayle. Photography by Ray Joyce. The Publisher would like to thank Accoutrement Kitchen stores at Chatswood and Mosman for their generosity in lending a large assortment of dishes used in the photographs.
Edited by Jennifer Partington
Designed by Ann Twells

CONTENTS

Introduction

The Barbecue Cookbook covers all aspects of barbecuing. It will appeal to all those who like the casual, outdoor way of life.

Barbecues are a good idea for everyday family meals and for parties when entertaining a large number of people. With a little organization, the food can be prepared in advance and everyone can relax together and have fun. Children will love helping with the cooking. All the dishes in this book can be actually cooked on a barbecue. There are limitless ideas for delicious meals, they vary from simple family fare to more sophisticated ideas for party food.

Pack up your portable barbecue, prepare and collect your food and go off into the country for an enjoyable relaxing day. Instead of serving barbecued chops or steaks once again, why not try barbecuing a chicken or freshly caught fish?

There are recipes for vegetables, salads and breads which are perfect accompaniments. There are also sauces, marinades and relishes which will add flavour to any barbecued food.

Children and teenagers love barbecue parties. Serve hamburgers, frankfurters or sausages in crusty rolls or ask the children to make up their own kebabs. There are recipes for tasty desserts to follow.

For a more festive occasion when entertaining a large number of people, barbecue a lamb or sucking pig. It is surprisingly easy and both are delicious to eat.

There is information here which will help you build and light your next barbecue fire and it is not difficult with these helpful hints.

The Barbecue Cookbook will certainly be a valuable addition to your collection of recipe books. Happy barbecuing!

THE BARBECUE

The Barbecue

To barbecue is to roast over an open fire. With a little thought and preparation, almost any meat or fish which can be cooked in an oven, can be barbecued.

Barbecues

There are innumerable designs to choose from, catering for every taste, purse and location. Barbecues have come a long way from the conventional brick and grill, wood or charcoal, home handy-man set-up.

With the innovation of gas and electric barbecues, the use of charcoal has become superfluous. "Volcanic rocks" are now a part of some electric barbecues. When heated they appear as natural charcoal, cooking your steaks with that unique barbecue flavour.

The range of barbecues available is not limited to the simple choice of whether a gas, electric or portable barbecue is required, but rather, whether alternative cooking methods such as bake, fry, rotisserie or casserole are desired.

One of the newer styles available is an enclosed, circular barbecue, which may be ignited by gas kettle or conventional charcoal. Its design is based on the assumption that the heat is rotated rather than the meat, thereby ensuring more even cooking and eliminating the risk of fire flare-ups.

Equipment

Basically, very little barbecue equipment is essential, but some items certainly make barbecuing easier. Ensure that the items you buy are sturdy in design and will stand up to rough treatment!

A long-handled pair of tongs and fork are basic necessities and a sturdy oven mit to protect the cook's hand is a good idea. Skewers are essential for testing foods and for barbecuing kebabs. These are made in various metals, stainless steel being extremely popular and practical. There are also shorter bamboo varieties which are ideal for seafood appetizers and fruit kebabs served as a dessert. Select bristle brushes for basting food. Small paint brushes are suitable, but do not choose any plastic or nylon varieties.

Marinades, oils and melted butter can be kept in fireproof pots by the barbecue. Hinged wire grills are essential when grilling over a bush barbecue as they can be turned easily when holding a number of chops, fish, frankfurters or hamburgers. Long-handled cast iron pots of various sizes, frying pans and skillets are handy for heating sauces, hotpots, frying fish and various meats. When buying plates, cutlery, glassware and table linen for barbecue parties, choose those which are sturdy and easy to look after. Bright colours promote a gay, casual atmosphere.

Aluminium foil is an extremely handy commodity when barbecuing. It can be used for wrapping potatoes, vegetables, bread, meat and fish. Use double foil to give extra strength and if foods to be barbecued are dry, grease foil with butter or oil. Food wrapped in foil may be placed directly in low coals or may be placed on grill or hotplate above hot coals. Wrap food in one of the following ways:

Tent wrap: Tear off desired length of aluminium foil. Place food to be wrapped in centre and bring two opposite edges together loosely across the top. Make a double or triple sealed edge, leaving enough room above and around the sides of the food for air to circulate freely. Triple fold ends flat. Food is thus wrapped in a loose wrap.

Bag wrap: Place food on a piece of aluminium foil. Bring all sides of foil up around food and seal by pressing all sides together by twisting top to close.

Building and Lighting your Fire

There are many theories as to the best method of starting a fire. Ease and quickness are essential factors. Charcoal, available in lump or briquette form, is definitely the quickest and easiest fuel to use in a barbecue. Certain types of dry, slow burning woods make good long-lasting coals and give a delicious flavour to barbecued foods.

When using wood, remember the fire must be prepared and lit well in advance so that by the time the barbecue is required for cooking, there are plenty of hot coals.

When using charcoal in your barbecue, soak a quantity of charcoal in methylated spirits for approximately three hours before the barbecue is to be lit. Place a layer of soaked charcoal in the barbecue then a layer of unsoaked charcoal on top. Alternatively, place charcoal to a depth of approximately two inches in the barbecue. On top, spaced approximately six inches apart, place firelighters (available at leading stores). Light fire and in approximately 45 minutes, when charcoal is covered with grey ash by day time or glows at night time, cooking may commence. Never use petrol or kerosine to help you light your fire.

For a bush barbecue, light the fire with paper, dry twigs and leaves. Add larger pieces of wood to the fire as it becomes established. Barbecuing may commence in approximately two hours or when there are plenty of hot glowing coals and the flames have disappeared. Once your fire is established, disturb it as little as possible. Constant poking and raking breaks up pockets of heat and lowers the temperature of the fire.

Use your hand to judge the heat of your fire. Hold your hand, palm towards the heat, near the grill level. If you have to withdraw your hand in less than three seconds, the coals are hot, approximately 200°C (400°F). If you can keep your hand at that level for three to four seconds, the coals are medium, approximately 180°C (350°F). For low coals, approximately 150°C (300°F), you should be able to keep your hand at grill level for four to five seconds.

Cooking on the Barbecue

The most important thing to remember when barbecuing is to barbecue with heat, not flames. The heat must be controlled so that the food is evenly cooked, not charred on the outside and raw inside.

Barbecue food 25 cm–40 cm (10 to 16 inches) away from the coals. Once the fire is evenly alight and ready for barbecuing, the heat may be controlled by the use of a hose fitted with a pressure reduction valve which gives a fine spray. This reduces the temperature of the fire quickly and cuts charcoal wastage. The water also prevents fat from food, such as sausages and steaks, from falling into the fire — this would accelerate the combustion of the charcoal and would be likely to burn the food being cooked. If the top of cooking food is sprayed with a fine spray of water, the globules of fat and water combine and explode into flame before touching the charcoal. It is a most effective way of controlling heat when barbecuing. Small pieces of food can be barbecued efficiently when this method is adopted. On the other hand, if more heat is required quickly when barbecuing, throw a few pieces of fat from the trimmed meat onto the charcoal or baste food with a little melted butter or oil, the dripping fat will activate the fire. When barbecuing is almost completed, try throwing a few gum leaves or herbs on the fire, it will give the food a delicious flavour.

Tips for Successful Barbecuing

● When a new barbecue has been purchased, read the manufacturer's instructions carefully before using. There may be certain tips which will be helpful.

● Many people line the firebox with doubled aluminium foil which reflects heat back to the food and therefore quickens cooking time. The foil also keeps your equipment clean.

● Vary the size of your fire depending on the amount of food to be cooked. Only make a small shallow fire to barbecue one steak or a few chops.

● Marinating meat before barbecuing adds flavour to your meat. It also tenderizes cheaper cuts of meat.

● Trim most fat from meat before barbecuing to prevent fat drippings from making the fire flare while cooking. Remaining fat should be snipped at regular intervals to prevent edges of meat from curling while cooking.

● Do not baste food with butter or oil while barbecuing as flames will burn the cooking food. Baste before and after the food is cooked.

● Use fat trimmed from meat for greasing hot plates and wire grills, this prevents meat from sticking.

● Aluminium foil trays and pans are handy for barbecues. Food can be kept warm in them, can be cooked in them or they can be used as serving dishes.

Appetizers

Start your next barbecue party with a delicious appetizer. A tasty morsel of food with which to begin the meal. Seafood kebabs, flavoursome meatballs and grilled grapefruit, all can be cooked successfully on a barbecue. Plan your next dinner menu in advance and the entire meal can be cooked and eaten out of doors.

When serving appetizers for a large number of people, make sure they are bite size, serve on large plates, place a cocktail stick in each and supply plenty of serviettes. Your party will be off to a good start.

Baked Grapefruit

FOR EACH SERVING:

½ grapefruit
1 tablespoon brown sugar
1 tablespoon sherry or rum
7.5 g (¼ oz) butter

Loosen grapefruit from skin with a small sharp knife. Remove centre core and separate segments. Sprinkle fruit with brown sugar and sherry and dot with butter.
Barbecue over hot coals for approximately 20 minutes or until grapefruit is warm through.
Note: To serve flaming, omit sherry and when grapefruit is warm, add 1 tablespoon rum, warm and ignite. Serve immediately.

Baked Oysters

SERVES: 4-6

24 oysters
MARINADE:
3 tablespoons oil
3 tablespoons lemon juice
½ teaspoon salt
freshly ground pepper
1 teaspoon dry mustard
½ teaspoon curry powder

Remove oysters from shells, place in marinade for approximately 30 minutes, turn once. Replace oysters in shells and pour a little of the marinade into each shell. Barbecue oysters over hot coals for approximately 10–15 minutes or until oysters are cooked.
Serve immediately.
Marinade: Combine all ingredients and mix together thoroughly.

Barbecued Meatballs

SERVES: 6

250 g (8 oz) finely minced steak
1 egg
1 teaspoon plain flour
1 tablespoon grated onion
¾ teaspoon salt
freshly ground pepper
60 g (2 oz) butter or margarine

Place all ingredients except butter in a mixing bowl and mix together thoroughly. Shape into 2.5 cm (1-inch) balls.
Heat butter in a heavy based frying pan or skillet and cook meatballs on barbecue over hot coals for approximately 20 minutes or until golden brown. Shake pan frequently to make sure meatballs are cooked on all sides.
Serve on cocktail sticks with Barbecue Sauce (see page 59) or Fresh Chutney (see page 62).

Grilled Ham and Cheese Rolls

FOR EACH SERVING:

1 slice ham
French mustard
1 slice processed Cheddar cheese
7.5 g (¼ oz) butter or margarine, melted

Spread ham thinly with French mustard and place a slice of cheese on top. Roll up and secure with cocktail sticks. Brush with butter and barbecue over medium hot coals for approximately 10 minutes, turn frequently and brush once or twice with butter while cooking. When ham is lightly browned and cheese begins to melt, remove cocktail sticks and serve immediately.

Chicken Liver Appetizers

MAKES: 16

1 x 470 g (15 oz) can artichoke hearts
French dressing (see page 63)
500 g (1 lb) chicken livers
250 g (8 oz) bacon rashers

Drain artichoke hearts, cut in halves, and marinate in French dressing for several hours. Wash chicken livers thoroughly and trim off threads and gall. Remove rind from bacon and cut rashers in halves.
Wrap chicken livers in pieces of bacon and secure with cocktail sticks. Spear half an artichoke heart onto the end of each cocktail stick.
Barbecue over hot coals for approximately 7–10 minutes or until chicken livers are cooked and bacon is lightly brown and crisp.
Variation: Small mushrooms, cleaned and trimmed, may replace the artichoke hearts.

Mushroom Buttons

Wash small mushrooms and remove stalks. Fill mushroom caps with pâté.
Melt butter in a heavy based frying pan or skillet and cook mushrooms over hot coals for approximately 10 minutes or until tender. Baste frequently with butter while cooking.
Fry small bacon rolls in the pan at the same time, until crisp and brown and serve with the mushrooms.

Scallop and Fruit Kebabs

(see photograph page 55)

Alternate scallops and pieces of firm banana or peach onto skewers. Brush with combined melted butter and lemon juice. Barbecue over hot coals for approximately 15–20 minutes or until scallops are tender. Be careful not to overcook scallops as they will become tough. Brush kebabs with melted butter and lemon juice again before serving.
Variation: Wrap the pieces of banana or peach in bacon before placing on skewers with scallops. Replace scallops with bite size pieces of any available fresh fish.

Prawn Kebabs

SERVES: 4
(see photograph page 55)

500 g (1 lb) green prawns (or shrimp)
6–8 rashers bacon
60 g (2 oz) butter or margarine, melted
¼ cup (2 fl oz) lemon juice

Shell and devein prawns. Remove rind from bacon and cut rashers in halves or thirds. Wrap each prawn in a piece of bacon and thread onto bamboo skewers. Combine melted butter and lemon juice and brush over kebabs.
Barbecue kebabs over hot coals for approximately 10–15 minutes or until prawns are cooked and bacon is lightly brown and crisp. Turn frequently while cooking and before serving, brush again with the melted butter and lemon juice. Pour any remaining butter into a small bowl or jug and serve with the kebabs.

Barbecued Meat

Nothing could be more tantalizing than the smell of barbecued meat — steaks, chops or tasty spareribs. Marinated beforehand, basted with your favourite sauce, all can be truly delicious. Barbecue individual pieces of meat or barbecue a joint whole, carve and serve with vegetables or salads. Barbecued meat is much tastier than the same meat cooked in an oven.

The art of barbecuing meat is to keep the juices in, not use them to feed the fire. Keep the meat a reasonable distance from the glowing coals and turn every few minutes. This keeps the juices running back and forth in the meat and away from the heat. You will find the meat is juicy when cooked this way.

Select a variety of mustards, relishes and sauces to accompany the barbecued meat.

Grilled meat, casseroles and foil wrapped chops are just a few of the delicious dishes to choose from.

Glazed Shoulder of Lamb

SERVES: 6-8

1 x 2 kg (4 lb) shoulder of lamb, boned, rolled and tied
1 teaspoon salt
¼ teaspoon pepper
GLAZE:
1 cup (8 fl oz) puréed apricots
¼ cup (3 oz) apple jelly
2 tablespoons finely chopped mint

Insert spit rod through centre of meat and secure. Rub with salt and pepper.
Place over medium hot coals. Cook for approximately 2–2½ hours or until tender. After meat has cooked for 1 hour, baste with glaze every 20 minutes.
Heat any remaining glaze and serve with the meat.
Glaze: Combine all ingredients and mix together thoroughly.

Roast Lamb and Pineapple Stuffing

SERVES: 6-8

1 x 2 kg (4 lb) leg of lamb, boned
salt and pepper
STUFFING:
1 x 470 g (15 oz) can crushed pineapple
1 cup (2 oz) soft white breadcrumbs
15 g (½ oz) butter, melted
1 tablespoon finely chopped parsley
½ teaspoon dried thyme
½ teaspoon dried marjoram
3 tablespoons milk
1 small onion, peeled, parboiled and chopped

Season meat with salt and pepper. Place stuffing on meat, roll up and tie securely with fine string.
Insert spit rod lengthways through centre of meat and secure.
Place over medium hot coals. Cook for approximately 2–2½ hours or until meat is tender. While cooking, baste with reserved pineapple juice.
Stuffing: Drain and reserve syrup from pineapple. Combine all ingredients and mix together thoroughly.

Grilled Lamb Chops and Cutlets

Choose leg, chump, loin, rib, forequarter or shoulder chops (or leg steak, sirloin, loin, rib, blade or arm chops).
Allow 1–2 chops for each person.
Trim excess fat from chops and barbecue over medium hot coals for approximately 10–15 minutes or until meat is tender and evenly brown on both sides.
While barbecuing, chops may be basted with favourite marinade or barbecue sauce.
If preferred, cook a loin of lamb whole. Ask your butcher to cut through the bone only, so that the chops can be cut with a knife when cooked.
Trim excess fat from loin and, turning frequently, barbecue over medium hot coals for approximately 45 minutes or until cooked as desired. By turning frequently, the meat juices will run up and down inside the meat and it will retain more moisture and will be pink and tender inside.
For a different flavour, insert fresh mint leaves, sprigs of fresh thyme or slivers of garlic between the chops before barbecuing.
To serve, carve into chops.

Lamb Chops Vermouth

SERVES: 4

8 lamb rib chops
MARINADE:
1 cup (8 fl oz) dry vermouth
1 cup (8 fl oz) salad oil
1 tablespoon lemon juice
1 onion, chopped
2 cloves garlic, crushed
1 teaspoon dried tarragon
1 teaspoon dried basil
1 teaspoon salt
10 peppercorns, crushed

Place lamb chops in a shallow dish and pour marinade over. Cover and stand for at least 4 hours, turn chops occasionally. Barbecue chops over medium hot coals for approximately 10–15 minutes. Baste with the marinade while cooking.
Serve when chops are tender and evenly brown.
Marinade: Combine all ingredients and mix together thoroughly.

Barbecued Butterfly Lamb

SERVES: 4-6
(see photograph page 37)

2½ kg (5 lb) leg of lamb, boned
3 cloves garlic, peeled
6 twigs of fresh rosemary
½ cup (4 fl oz) lemon juice
milled pepper and coarse salt
salad oil

Flatten boned lamb into a good shape and use two long metal skewers to insert into the lamb to form a 'cross' to keep lamb in good shape during the barbecuing. Make a few slits into the meat and add a piece of garlic and a piece of rosemary. Marinate lamb with lemon juice, pepper, salt and some oil, turning often for 2 hours. Ensure that the barbecue fire has even, glowing coals and not a fierce flame. Cook for 1 hour, turning the lamb often and spooning over the marinade during the cooking. Add light twigs to the fire towards the final cooking to give crisp browning if desired. The lamb should be slightly pink, carved thinly and served with Tabbouleh salad on Lebanese flat bread.

Barbecued Lamb

SERVES: 6-8

1 x 3 kg (6 lb) leg of lamb, boned
MARINADE:
1 cup (8 fl oz) olive oil
¼ cup (2 fl oz) wine vinegar
1 small onion, chopped
2 cloves garlic, crushed
freshly ground black pepper
1 teaspoon salt
sprig of rosemary

Beat lamb with a meat mallet to flatten. Place in a shallow dish and pour over marinade. Cover and stand for several hours, turn occasionally.
Drain and barbecue meat over medium hot coals for approximately 2 hours or until meat is tender, turn frequently and baste with Barbecue Sauce (see page 59) while cooking.
To serve, carve into thick slices.
Marinade: Combine all ingredients and mix together thoroughly.

Devilled American Pork Ribs

SERVES: 6
(see photograph page 19)

1 kg (2 lb) American Pork Ribs from rib loin
½ cup (4 fl oz) tomato sauce
2 tablespoons malt vinegar
2 teaspoons brown sugar
2 tablespoons Worcestershire sauce
1 small grated onion
1 clove garlic crushed
1 teaspoon salt
dash chilli powder

If desired, cut ribs into short pieces or keep in a rack. Place remaining ingredients into a blender and mix well together. Pour over pork ribs, brushing on well. Allow to marinate for several hours spooning mixture over pork and turning often. Cook ribs on a barbecue with glowing coals for approximately 30 minutes, brushing over the marinade during the cooking. Turn pork often and serve with Chilli con Carne and crusty French bread.

Chilli Con Carne

SERVES: 4-6
(see photograph page 19)

1 onion, chopped
2 cloves garlic, crushed
1 tablespoon oil
500 g (1 lb) minced steak
1 x 470 g (15 oz) can condensed tomato soup
1 teaspoon salt
1 tablespoon chilli powder
½ cup (4 fl oz) water
1 green pepper, seeded and chopped
2 cups cooked red kidney beans or
    2 x 375 g (12 oz) cans kidney beans, drained

Sauté onion and garlic in hot oil in a large heavy based frying pan. Add minced beef and cook until meat browns, stir continuously. Add soup, salt, chilli powder and water. Cover and simmer for 10 minutes, stir occasionally.
Add green pepper and beans, simmer for a further 20 minutes and serve hot.
Serve with boiled rice.

Devilled American Pork Ribs and Chille Con Carne (see above)

Pineapple Barbecued Lamb Shanks

SERVES: 4

8 lamb shanks
1 x 470 g (15 oz) can pineapple slices
MARINADE:
1 cup (8 fl oz) pineapple juice
2 teaspoons curry powder
3 tablespoons brown sugar
1 clove garlic, crushed
1 teaspoon salt
freshly ground black pepper
3 tablespoons salad oil

Wipe shanks with a damp cloth and place them in a single layer in a glass, earthenware or enamel dish. Mix marinade ingredients, adding to them the liquid drained from the pineapple slices. (Store slices in an air-tight plastic container in refrigerator until barbecue time.) Pour marinade over shanks and marinate for at least 4 hours, turning them occasionally.
To barbecue, place shanks over glowing coals and cook for 25–30 minutes, turning often and basting with marinade. Place pineapple slices on barbecue 5 minutes before shanks are cooked.
Garnish with barbecued pineapple slices. Serve with salad and French bread and butter.

Indian Spiced Mutton

SERVES: 6

1 kg (2 lb) finely minced mutton
½ cup (2 oz) dry breadcrumbs
1 egg
salt and pepper
2 teaspoons garam marsala
12 prunes, pitted

Place all ingredients except prunes in a mixing bowl. Mix together thoroughly and shape into 12 croquettes or rissoles, placing a prune in the centre of each.
Barbecue over hot coals for approximately 10–15 minutes or until cooked.
If desired, baste with favourite marinade while cooking.

Bush Barbecue

SERVES: 4–8

4 grilling steaks (T-bone, rump or cross-cut blade)
4–8 lamb chops (short loin or forequarter)
4–8 thick sausages
commercial barbecue sauce
salt
mustard
salad vegetables
MARINADE:
1 cup (8 fl oz) red wine
½ cup (4 fl oz) oil
1 small onion, sliced
1 garlic clove, crushed
1 crumbled bay leaf
2 sprigs each thyme and parsley
freshly ground black pepper

Place steaks and chops in a plastic container with a good seal. Combine marinade ingredients, pour over meats, seal and refrigerate for several hours. Turn container over occasionally to redistribute marinade.
Place sausages in cold water to cover, slowly bring to simmering point, leave off heat for 10 minutes, drain and store in a sealed container in refrigerator.
Pack containers of meats and salad ingredients in a portable insulated cooler with ice. Don't forget remaining ingredients (plus tongs, a brush, the billy can and tea).
To cook meats have fire at glowing coals stage, put meats on grid and baste steaks and chops with marinade, sausages with barbecue sauce.
Cook until done to taste, turning with tongs. Season with salt.
Serve with salad vegetables, mustard, crusty bread rolls and billy tea.

A Grilled Hamburger is a favourite at any time (see page 32).

Barbecued Steaks

Rather than cutting steaks into individual portions and cooking these separately, try cooking steaks in large slices and then cutting the cooked steaks into serving portions. Steak should be well trimmed and all excess fat removed. Barbecue rump steak (or sirloin steak) over medium coals for approximately 45 minutes–1 hour, according to taste. Cook boned sirloin steak (or boned rib steak) over slow coals for approximately 1½–2 hours, according to taste. Cook fillet steak (or tenderloin steak) over medium coals for 30–45 minutes, according to taste.

When individual steaks are barbecued, cook over medium hot coals for approximately 10–20 minutes, depending on whether steak is to be served rare, medium or well done.

It is important to remember to turn the steak frequently while cooking so that the juices are retained inside the meat. Should you leave the meat without turning for some time, you will notice a quantity of blood on top, whereas by turning the meat frequently, the juices run up and down inside the meat and it will remain moist. The steak may be smeared with pâté, horseradish relish or mustard to add flavour while cooking.

To serve, carve steak and either place on dinner plates or for a buffet dinner party, serve on slices of French bread.

Barbecued Sirloin Steaks

6 x 250 g (8 oz) sirloin steaks (or rib steaks)
SAUCE:
1 can beer
1 tablespoon chilli sauce
¼ cup (2 fl oz) salad oil
2 tablespoons soy sauce
1 tablespoon French mustard
½ teaspoon Tabasco sauce
1 onion, chopped
2 cloves garlic, crushed
salt and pepper

Brush meat with sauce.
Barbecue over medium hot coals for 10–20 minutes, according to taste. Baste occasionally with the sauce while cooking. Heat the remaining sauce and serve with the steak.
Sauce: Combine all ingredients and mix together thoroughly.

Ginger Steak

SERVES: 6

6 pieces porterhouse steak
30 g (1 oz) butter, melted
MARINADE:
¼ cup (2 fl oz) soy sauce
½ cup (4 fl oz) pineapple juice
1 tablespoon ground ginger
2 tablespoons dry sherry
½ teaspoon dry mustard
1 clove garlic, crushed

Place steak in a large shallow dish. Pour marinade over, cover and stand for at least 4 hours.
Drain meat and barbecue over medium hot coals for 10–20 minutes, according to taste. Baste occasionally with melted butter while cooking.
Heat remaining marinade and pour over steak before serving.
Marinade: Combine all ingredients and mix together thoroughly.

Grilled Steak and Wine Sauce

SERVES: 4–6

4–6 T-bone or porterhouse steaks
1 tablespoon finely chopped onion
30 g (1 oz) butter or margarine
1 tablespoon plain flour
¼ cup (2 fl oz) water
¾ cup (6 fl oz) claret
salt and pepper
¼ cup chopped parsley

Barbecue steaks over medium hot coals for 10–20 minutes, according to taste. In the meantime, cok onion in butter until golden brown. Mix flour and water until smooth, add to the onion mixture, add the claret. Bring to the boil, stirring continuously. Season to taste with salt and pepper and simmer for 10 minutes. Add the parsley and serve immediately with the grilled steaks.

Quick Garlic Steaks

SERVES: 6-8

6-8 pieces fillet steak, 2.5 cm (1-inch) thick
   (or tenderloin steak)
60 g (2 oz) butter or margarine, melted
1 clove garlic, crushed
juice of 2 lemons
2 tablespoons Worcestershire sauce
salt
freshly ground pepper

Cut steaks almost through the centre and
open out. Beat steaks with a meat mallet
until 5 mm (¼-inch) thick. Combine melted
butter and garlic, dip steaks in butter to
coat.
Barbecue steaks over medium hot coals for
5-15 minutes, according to taste. Baste
while cooking with garlic butter.
Add lemon juice, Worcestershire sauce and
salt and pepper to remaining garlic butter,
mix well and pour over steaks before
serving.

Steak with Blue Cheese

SERVES: 4

4 pieces rump steak (or sirloin steak)
60 g (2 oz) butter, softened
60 g (2 oz) blue vein cheese
2 tablespoons finely chopped parsley
freshly ground pepper
extra 30 g (1 oz) butter, melted
1 teaspoon Worcestershire sauce

Make a slit in each steak, parallel to the
surface of the meat.
Cream softened butter with blue vein
cheese and parsley, place inside pocket of
each steak. Sprinkle steaks with pepper.
Mix extra butter and Worcestershire sauce
together.
Barbecue steaks over medium hot coals for
10-20 minutes, according to taste. Baste
with the butter mixture occasionally while
cooking.

Marinated Barbecue Steaks or Chops

SERVES: 4

4 cross-cut blade steaks or lamb
   forequarter chops
SOY MARINADE:
½ cup (4 fl oz) soy sauce
1 clove garlic, finely chopped
freshly ground black pepper

Place steak or chops in a large mixing
bowl. Mix marinade ingredients and pour
over meat and marinate for at least 30
minutes. Lift meat out of marinade and
drain a little.
Place meat on barbecue over glowing coals
and cook for 3-4 minutes on each side, or
less if you prefer medium rare meat.
Serve with barbecued sauce, salad,
buttered bread rolls or foil-baked jacket
potatoes.

Barbecue Beef Feast

SERVES: 4-6
(see photograph page 37)

1 x 2 kg (4 lb) piece beef (bolar or oyster
   blade)
1 tablespoon mixed French mustard
2 cloves garlic
2 tablespoons cracked or milled
   peppercorns
1 tablespoon fresh mixed herbs

Trim piece of beef into a flat, thick shape.
Mix mustard with crushed garlic,
peppercorns and herbs. Spread over the
meat, cover and let stand for 1 hour. Ensure
a barbecue fire with even heat of glowing
coals and place meat on a greased
hot-plate and cook on all sides to sear the
meat well. Continue to cook to desired
stage so that the centre is just pink. Test
the internal juices as a guide. Allow
approximately one hour for cooking,
depending on the fire and the thickness of
meat. Remove to a warm part of the fire
and cover with foil and stand for
approximately 10 minutes before carving.
Serve with Tossed Green Salad (see page
54) and Baked Potatoes (see page 53), with
sour cream and chopped chives.
Serve a selection of mustard, relish and
tasty sauces to add to beef when serving.

Sesame Flavoured Steak

SERVES: 4

4 T-bone steaks, 1 cm (½ inch) thick, or
    sirloin, porterhouse or Scotch fillet
MARINADE:
2 tablespoons salad oil
1 teaspoon lemon juice
¼ cup (2 fl oz) soy sauce
1 tablespoon brown sugar
2 tablespoons grated onion or chopped
    spring onions
freshly ground black pepper
¼ teaspoon garlic powder
¼ teaspoon ground ginger
pinch of monosodium glutamate
2 tablespoons sesame seeds

Place steak in a flat dish. Combine
marinade ingredients and pour over
steaks. Marinate for 1 hour, turning steaks
two or three times.
To barbecue, lift steak from marinade and
place over glowing coals. Cook for 6–8
minutes on each side, according to taste
and type of steak used. Brush with
marinade during cooking.
Serve with salads, baked jacket potatoes
and garlic bread.

Peppered Pork

SERVES: 6

6 thin pork loin chops
30 g (1 oz) butter, melted
1 teaspoon salt
1 tablespoon black peppercorns, crushed
¼ cup (3 oz) blackcurrant jelly
12 canned peach halves

Brush the chops with melted butter and
sprinkle with salt. Press the crushed
peppercorns evenly into the chops.
Barbecue over medium coals for
approximately 15–20 minutes. Place a
spoonful of blackcurrant jelly in each
peach half and place on side of barbecue
to warm through.
When pork chops are tender and evenly
brown, serve with the warmed peach
halves.

Pork and Apple

FOR EACH SERVING:
1 pork leg chop (or fresh ham centre slice)
½ cooking apple
salt and pepper
½ tablespoon finely chopped fresh sage
2 tablespoons cider or 1 tablespoon cider
    and 1 tablespoon cream

Remove excess fat from chop. Place on
large piece of greased, doubled aluminium
foil. Peel, core and thinly slice the apple
and place over chop. Sprinkle with
seasonings. Turn sides of foil up and add
cider. Seal foil securely.
Cook on barbecue over hot coals for
approximately 1–1¼ hours or until meat is
tender.

Whole Loin of Pork

Ask butcher to cut through bone only, so
that chops can be cut with a knife when
cooked. Rub salt into skin of pork to make
good crackling. Slivers of garlic may be
inserted between the chops if desired.
Barbecue over medium coals for
approximately 45 minutes–1 hour or until
meat is tender. Barbecue on the bone side
mainly and cut down cooking time on the
skin side.
Watch pork carefully while barbecuing so
that the crackling does not catch and burn.
To serve, carve into individual chops.

Barbecue Spareribs

SERVES: 6

1 kg (2 lb) Pork Spareribs or slices from
    loin belly
2 tablespoons soy sauce
2 tablespoons sherry
2 teaspoons Chinese Hoisin sauce
2 cloves garlic crushed
1 tablespoon honey
½ teaspoon Chinese Five Spice

Trim pork and cut into chunky size pieces
if very large. Combine remaining
ingredients into a shallow dish. Add pork
pieces and coat well. Allow to marinate for
1 hour or more.
Barbecue the spareribs on a hot-plate,
turning often to cook evenly and brush with
marinade if crusty texture is desired.
Depending on fire and heat, cook for
approximately 20 minutes.

Ham and Pineapple

SERVES: 6

6 slices cooked ham, 1 cm (½-inch) thick
6 slices fresh or canned pineapple
GLAZE:
½ cup (5 oz) honey
¼ cup (2 fl oz) lemon juice
½ teaspoon ground cloves
2 teaspoons soy sauce

Barbecue ham and pineapple quickly over hot coals, basting frequently with the glaze. Serve when warmed through and lightly brown.
Glaze: Combine all ingredients and mix together thoroughly.

Veal Chops

FOR EACH SERVING:

1 veal loin chop
1 tomato, skinned and chopped
½ tablespoon finely chopped onion
½ tablespoon finely chopped chives
pinch of dried tarragon
pinch of dried marjoram
2 tablespoons finely chopped cucumber
  with peel
salt and pepper
1 tablespoon oil
1 tablespoon sherry

Place chop on large piece of doubled aluminium foil. Add remaining ingredients, turning sides of foil up before adding the oil and sherry. Seal foil securely.
Place packages on barbecue over medium hot coals and cook for approximately 30 minutes or until meat is tender. Turn once while cooking.

Veal Cutlets

FOR EACH SERVING:

2 veal cutlets (or veal rib chops)
4 mushrooms
2 tablespoons white wine
2 tablespoons cream
salt and pepper
1 tablespoon finely chopped chives

Place cutlets side by side in centre of a large piece of greased, doubled aluminium foil. Peel and slice mushrooms thinly, place on top of cutlets. Turn up sides of foil. Add wine, cream, salt and pepper and chives. Seal foil securely.
Place packages on barbecue over medium hot coals and cook for approximately 30 minutes or until meat is tender. Turn once while cooking.

Barbecued Liver and Bacon

SERVES: 4-6

1 lamb's liver
4-6 rashers bacon, rind removed
MARINADE:
⅓ cup (2 fl oz) olive oil
juice of 1 lemon
salt
freshly ground pepper
1 tablespoon finely chopped parsley

Soak liver in water for 1 hour. Remove skin and cut out tubes. Cut into 1 cm (½-inch) slices, with knife in a slanting position. Place liver in a shallow dish, pour over marinade, cover and stand for 1 hour. Drain liver and barbecue over medium hot coals for approximately 10-12 minutes. Grill bacon until crisp and brown. Heat remaining marinade and serve with liver and bacon.
Marinade: Combine all ingredients and mix together thoroughly.

Kebabs

A meal on a stick! Steak, veal, lamb, pork, poultry and seafood, all are suitable for kebabs. The combination of ingredients is innumerable and you can make up your own variations to suit family and friends.

Cheaper cuts of meat can be utilized. By cutting meat into bite size pieces and placing in a marinade for several hours before barbecuing, coarser grained meats become tender and tasty. Baste kebabs with melted butter, oil, your favourite sauce or any remaining marinade. Remember to cut firmer ingredients into smaller pieces than the softer ones. For example, buy small cherry tomatoes and use them whole, but cut onions and peppers into pieces so that all ingredients will be cooked at the same time. In fact, some people like to parboil onions and peppers before barbecuing.

For a main course, make long kebabs on stainless steel skewers and serve on a bed of boiled rice or pilaf. For an appetizer, make smaller kebabs on bamboo skewers and serve directly from the grill.

For an informal barbecue party, prepare ingredients and place in large colourful bowls, ask guests to make up their own kebabs. Serve with crisp salads, pickles and relishes. Hot crusty bread is also a good accompaniment.

Chicken and Orange Kebabs

SERVES: 4

3 oranges
3-6 rashers bacon
500 g (1 lb) cooked chicken
24 small mushroom caps, peeled
60 g (2 oz) butter or margarine
BASTING SAUCE:
juice of 1 large orange
extra 60 g (2 oz) butter or margarine,
    melted

Peel oranges, remove pith and divide into segments. Remove rind from bacon, fry gently and cut into 2.5 cm (1-inch) pieces. Remove skin from chicken and cut into 2.5 cm (1-inch) cubes. Sauté mushroom caps lightly in butter.
Alternate orange segments, bacon, chicken and mushroom caps onto skewers.
Barbecue kebabs over hot coals, turn and baste frequently with the sauce while cooking.
Serve when kebabs are warmed through and lightly browned on all sides.
Basting sauce: Mix orange juice and melted butter together.

Veal Kebabs in Chinese Marinade

SERVES: 6

1 kg (2 lb) boneless leg veal, cut into
    2.5 cm (1-inch) pieces
MARINADE:
½ cup (4 fl oz) soy sauce
¼ cup (2 fl oz) salad oil
1 teaspoon ground ginger
1 teaspoon dry mustard
1 teaspoon sugar
3 cloves garlic, crushed

Place meat in a mixing bowl, pour over marinade, cover and stand for 2-3 hours. Drain meat and thread onto skewers. Barbecue over hot coals for approximately 20 minutes or until meat is tender. Turn and baste frequently with the marinade while cooking.
Marinade: Combine all ingredients and mix together thoroughly.

Minted Lamb Kebabs

SERVES: 4

1 kg (2 lb) lean lamb, cut into 3.5 cm
    (1½-inch) cubes
8 small tomatoes
12 small mushrooms
MARINADE:
2 tablespoons chopped fresh mint
½ cup (4 fl oz) vinegar
2½ tablespoons brown sugar
pinch of dry mustard
½ teaspoon salt
60 g (2 oz) butter
1 teaspoon grated lemon rind
¼ cup (2 fl oz) white wine

Place meat in a bowl, add marinade and mix well. Cover and stand for 1-2 hours. Drain meat and alternate meat, tomatoes and mushrooms onto skewers.
Barbecue over hot coals for approximately 20 minutes, turning and basting frequently with marinade while cooking.
Marinade: Place all ingredients except white wine in saucepan. Bring to the boil, take off heat and allow to stand for 30 minutes, add white wine.

Lamb Kidney Kebabs

Allow 3 kidneys and 3 bacon rashers for each person.
Wash and skin kidneys, cut in halves and remove cores. Cut rind from bacon and cut each rasher in half. Wrap each piece around a piece of kidney, place on skewers.
Barbecue over hot coals for approximately 15-20 minutes or until kidneys are cooked and bacon is crisp and brown. Turn kebabs frequently while cooking.
Variations: Replace kidney with pieces of lamb's fry, cooked brain or sweetbread.

Armenian Shish Kebabs

SERVES: 6

1 kg (2 lb) lean lamb, cut into 3.5 cm
   (1½-inch) cubes
1 green pepper, seeded
1 red pepper, seeded
12 small white onions, halved
MARINADE:
½ cup (4 fl oz) salad oil
¼ cup (2 fl oz) lemon juice
1 teaspoon salt
½ teaspoon dried marjoram
½ teaspoon dried thyme
freshly ground pepper
1 clove garlic, crushed
½ cup chopped onion
2 tablespoons chopped parsley

Place meat in a mixing bowl and pour over
the marinade. Mix well, cover and stand for
at least 3–4 hours.
Cut peppers into 3.5 cm (1½-inch) pieces.
Drain meat and place on skewers
alternating with pieces of pepper and
halved onions.
Barbecue over hot coals for approximately
20 minutes or until meat is tender. Turn
kebabs frequently and baste with the
marinade while cooking
Marinade: Combine all ingredients and
mix together thoroughly.

Mexican Steak Kebabs

SERVES: 4–5

750 g (1½ lb) round steak, cut into 3.5 cm
   (1½-inch) cubes
MEXICAN SAUCE:
½ cup chopped onion
1 tablespoon olive oil
1 cup (8 fl oz) red wine vinegar
½ teaspoon salt
½ teaspoon dried oregano
½ teaspoon dried cummin
½ teaspoon ground cloves
½ teaspoon ground cinnamon
½ teaspoon pepper
1 clove garlic, crushed

Place meat on skewers.
Baste with sauce and barbecue over hot
coals for approximately 12–15 minutes or
until meat is tender. Turn frequently and
baste with the sauce while cooking.
Mexican sauce: Combine all ingredients
and mix together thoroughly.

Steak Combination Kebabs

SERVES: 4

750 g (1½ lb) lean rump steak (or sirloin
   steak)
12 small onions
2 green peppers
12 small tomatoes
60 g (2 oz) butter, melted

Cut steak into 3.5 cm (1½-inch) cubes.
Parboil onions. Seed peppers and cut into
3.5 cm (1½-inch) pieces. Alternate steak,
onions, pieces of pepper and tomatoes onto
skewers. Baste with melted butter.
Barbecue over hot coals for approximately
12–15 minutes or until meat is tender. Turn
kebabs frequently and baste with melted
butter again before serving.

Steak and Pineapple Kebabs

SERVES: 4–6
(see photograph page 55)

750 g (1½ lb) lean rump steak (or sirloin
   steak), cut into 2.5 cm (1-inch) cubes
250 g (8 oz) button mushrooms
1 green pepper, seeded
1 x 470 g (15 oz) can pineapple pieces or
chunks of fresh pineapple
MARINADE:
2 cups (16 fl oz) tomato juice
½ cup (4 fl oz) vinegar
2 tablespoons French mustard
1 tablespoon sugar
2 teaspoons salt
freshly ground pepper

Place steak in a mixing bowl, pour over
marinade. Mix well, cover and stand for 2
hours.
Peel mushrooms and remove stalks. Cut
pepper into 2.5 cm (1-inch) pieces. Drain
pineapple pieces. Drain meat and
alternate meat, mushrooms, pepper and
pineapple pieces onto skewers.
Barbecue over hot coals, turning and
basting frequently with marinade while
cooking. Cook for approximately 12–15
minutes or until meat is tender.
Marinade: Combine all ingredients and
mix together thoroughly.

Steak and Lobster Kebabs

SERVES: 6-8

1 large green lobster
2 green peppers
750 g (1½ lb) lean rump steak (or sirloin steak), cut into 3.5 cm (1½-inch) cubes
SAUCE:
¼ cup (2 fl oz) Sauterne
¼ cup (2 fl oz) lemon juice
¼ cup (2 fl oz) salad oil

Remove meat from tail of lobster, cut into 3.5 cm (1½-inch) chunks. Seed peppers and cut into 3.5 cm (1½-inch) pieces. Alternate steak, lobster and pieces of pepper onto skewers.
Barbecue over hot coals for approximately 12-15 minutes or until meat and lobster are tender. Turn frequently and baste with sauce while cooking.
Sauce: Combine all ingredients and mix together thoroughly.

Satay

SERVES: 3-4

500 g (1 lb) chicken breasts, cut into 2.5 cm (1 inch) cubes
MARINADE:
1 teaspoon soy sauce
1 teaspoon Tabasco sauce
1 tablespoon white vinegar
2 tablespoons salad oil
1 tablespoon brown sugar
1 clove garlic, crushed

Place in a mixing bowl, pour over marinade and mix thoroughly, cover and stand for 3-4 hours.
Place chicken on fine skewers and barbecue over hot coals for approximately 5 minutes or until meat is cooked , turn frequently.
Marinade: Combine all ingredients and mix thoroughly.

Teriyaki Kebabs

SERVES: 4

500 g (1 lb) rump steak cut 2.5 cm (1-inch) thick (round steak may be used)
1 x 470 g (15 oz) can pineapple pieces
stuffed olives
MARINADE:
¼ cup (2 fl oz) soy sauce
1 tablespoon dry white wine or lemon juice
1 clove garlic, finely chopped
1 tablespoon oil

Trim excess fat from steak and cut into long strips 8-10 cm (3-4 inches long and 5 mm (¼ inch) wide. For easier slicing partially freeze meat. Mix marinade ingredients in a mixing bowl, add steak strips and coat well with marinade. Leave to stand for ½ hour. Marinate round steak for 3 hours.
To prepare kebabs, take out strips of steak and drain. Weave each strip onto a skewer, piercing an olive or a pineapple chunk onto a skewer each time you pass it through the meat. To fill skewer, a second piece of steak may be needed. This quantity should fill at least six skewers.
Place over glowing coals and barbecue quickly, turning often, and brushing with marinade.
Garnish with pineapple and parsley sprigs. Serve with rice or noodles and tossed green salad.

Vegetable Kebabs

Spear a selection of vegetables onto skewers and serve with grilled steak, chops or sausages. Try small tomatoes, mushroom caps, chunks of fresh pineapple, parboiled corncobs (cut into 2.5 cm (1-inch) rings) and small parboiled onions.
Barbecue over medium coals, turning frequently and basting with melted butter or margarine while cooking.

Pork and Apricot Kebabs

SERVES: 6-8

1 kg (2 lb) boneless shoulder pork
250 g (8 oz) dried apricots
Marsala
MARINADE:
1 cup (8 fl oz) pineapple juice
½ cup (4 fl oz) soy sauce
1 clove garlic, crushed
2 teaspoons chopped preserved ginger

Cut pork into 3.5 cm (1½-inch) cubes and place in a mixing bowl, pour over marinade, mix well and cover. Stand for 1 hour. Place dried apricots in another bowl, cover with Marsala and stand for 1 hour. Drain meat and apricots and place alternately on skewers.
Barbecue over hot coals for approximately 20–25 minutes or until meat is tender. Turn frequently and baste with the marinade while cooking.
Marinade: Combine all ingredients and mix together thoroughly.
Variation: Replace pork with pieces of lamb.

Polynesian Pork Kebabs

SERVES: 4

750 g (1½ lb) boneless leg pork
MARINADE:
1 finely chopped onion
1-2 cloves garlic, crushed
4 Brazil nuts, grated
¼ cup (2 fl oz) lemon juice
¼ cup (2 fl oz) soy sauce
1 teaspoon pepper
few drops Tabasco sauce
1 teaspoon ground coriander
2 tablespoons brown sugar
2 tablespoons salad oil

Cut pork into 2.5 cm (1-inch) cubes. Place meat in a mixing bowl, pour over marinade, mix well, cover and stand for at least 2 hours. Drain meat and place on skewers.
Barbecue over hot coals for approximately 20–25 minutes or until meat is tender. While cooking, baste frequently with marinade and turn regularly.
Heat any remaining marinade and serve with the kebabs.
Marinade: Combine all ingredients and mix together thoroughly.

Barbecued Burgers

Hamburgers are a delicious favourite with young and old. Seasoned with salt and pepper and barbecued directly over glowing coals or on a skillet or hotplate, nothing could be more tasty. They are ideal for a large group of friends as they can be prepared in advance and guests can add their own accompaniments depending on their individual tastes.

Buy freshly minced steak or ask your butcher to mince your favourite cut of steak specially for you. If the steak is particularly lean, add some shredded suet to the meat mixture before shaping the hamburgers, they will be moist and tender when cooked. Roll the prepared mince out to the desired thickness and cut into rounds a little larger than the bread rolls to be filled. The hamburgers will shrink slightly while cooking. For a smaller number of people you may like to serve thicker hamburgers shaped individually. Place a layer on a tray, cover with clear plastic wrap or aluminium foil and place another layer on top. Place in refrigerator until ready to cook.

Barbecued hamburgers should be juicy and tender when cooked, serve between thick slices of fresh bread or toast or serve in hamburger rolls. Bread and rolls may be spread with butter or mayonnaise. Add a fried egg or grilled bacon for extra nourishment for children. Serve relishes, mustards, pickles and salad ingredients in separate bowls and ask guests to help themselves.

Grilled Hamburgers

SERVES: 6
(see photograph page 20)

750 g (1½ lb) finely minced steak
1 onion, finely chopped
1 teaspoon salt
freshly ground pepper
6 hamburger rolls, split, toasted and
    buttered
BARBECUE SAUCE:
1 cup (8 fl oz) tomato sauce
2 teaspoons Worcestershire sauce
½ teaspoon celery salt
few drops chilli sauce

Combine minced steak, onion and
seasonings in a mixing bowl, mix together
thoroughly. Shape into 6 hamburgers,
approximately 1 cm (½-inch) thick.
Barbecue over hot coals for approximately
8–10 minutes on each side or until cooked.
Baste hamburgers with the barbecue sauce
while cooking.
Place hamburgers in toasted rolls with
selection of salad greens, tomato, beetroot,
sliced onions and sliced gherkins and top
with extra sauce or mustard if desired.
Barbecue sauce: Combine all ingredients
and mix together thoroughly.

Hawaiian Hamburgers

SERVES: 8

1 kg (2 lb) finely minced steak
1 egg
1 onion, finely chopped
½ cup (2 oz) dry breadcrumbs
2 tablespoons tomato sauce
2 tablespoons brown sugar
1 teaspoon French mustard
1 teaspoon salt
commercial barbecue sauce
8 slices fresh or canned pineapple

Combine minced steak, egg, onion,
breadcrumbs, tomato sauce, sugar,
mustard and seasonings in a mixing bowl.
Mix together thoroughly and shape into 8
hamburgers.
Barbecue over hot coals for approximately
8–10 minutes on each side or until cooked.
While cooking, brush occasionally with
barbecue sauce.
Barbecue slices of pineapple until golden
brown, top each hamburger with a slice
and serve immediately.

Wine Hamburgers

SERVES: 8

1 kg (2 lb) finely minced steak
1 cup (4 oz) soft white breadcrumbs
1 egg
¼ cup (2 fl oz) Burgundy
1 onion, finely chopped
1 teaspoon salt
freshly ground pepper
8 thick slices French bread, cut diagonally
    and buttered
BURGUNDY SAUCE:
60 g (2 oz) butter or margarine
1 large onion, finely chopped
¼ cup (2 fl oz) Burgundy

Combine minced steak, breadcrumbs, egg,
Burgundy, onion and seasonings in a
mixing bowl. Mix together thoroughly and
shape into 8 hamburgers, approximately
2.5 cm (1-inch) thick.
Brush with the sauce and barbecue over
hot coals for approximately 8–10 minutes on
each side or until cooked, brush
occasionally with the sauce while cooking.
Serve on the buttered French bread.
Burgundy sauce: Melt butter in a
saucepan, add onion and cook until golden
and transparent, add Burgundy and
simmer for 5 minutes.

Pizza Burgers

SERVES: 6

750g (1½ lb) finely minced steak
⅓ cup (1½ oz) grated Parmesan cheese
¼ cup finely chopped onion
¼ cup chopped green olives
1 teaspoon salt
freshly ground pepper
1 teaspoon dried oregano
1 x 185 g (6 oz) can tomato paste
6 slices Mozzarella cheese
6 slices tomato
6 hamburger rolls, split, toasted and
    spread with mayonnaise

Combine minced steak, Parmesan cheese,
onion, olives, seasonings and tomato paste
in a mixing bowl, mix together thoroughly.
Shape into 8 hamburgers and barbecue
over hot coals for approximately 10
minutes, turn. Top each hamburger with a
slice of Mozzarella cheese and tomato.
Barbecue for a further 5 minutes or until
hamburgers are cooked.
Serve in prepared rolls.

Surprise Hamburgers

SERVES: 8

1 kg (2 lb) finely minced steak
2 eggs
½ cup (1 oz) soft white breadcrumbs
1 teaspoon salt
freshly ground pepper
8 hamburger rolls, buttered
FILLINGS:
8 slices processed Cheddar cheese, spread
   with mustard or fruit chutney
8 thin slices onion, spread with chilli sauce
8 slices tomato, spread with mayonnaise
   and sprinkled with chopped chives
8 slices ham, spread with French mustard
sliced dill pickles
Horseradish relish

Combine minced steak, eggs, breadcrumbs
and seasonings in a mixing bowl. Mix
together thoroughly and shape into 16 thin
patties. Place chosen filling on 8 of the
patties, top with remaining patties and
press edges together firmly. Barbecue over
hot coals for approximately 8–10 minutes on
each side or until cooked.
Serve in buttered rolls.

Sausages and Frankfurters

There are innumerable types of sausages and frankfurters available. Adapt any of the following recipes using your favourite type.

Sausages and frankfurters are firm favourites with children and teenagers and they are an economical meal for a large number of guests. They can be included in casseroles which can be prepared in advance in the kitchen or they can be cooked directly on the barbecue grill. Sausages may be parboiled before barbecuing, perhaps a little flavour is lost but there is less likelihood of sausages being raw inside or bursting while cooking. If sausages are barbecued raw, cook over medium coals, turning frequently until they are cooked through and evenly brown outside.

Barbecued Bratwurst Sausages

SERVES: 4-5

500 g (1 lb) bratwurst sausages
2 cans beer
1 onion, thinly sliced
1 teaspoon Worcestershire sauce

Place all ingredients in a heavy based saucepan or flameproof casserole. Bring to simmering point and simmer gently for approximately 5 minutes, drain.
Barbecue sausages, turning frequently, for approximately 10 minutes or until evenly brown.

Italian Style Frankfurters

SERVES: 4-5

250 g (8 oz) minced steak
½ cup chopped onion
½ cup chopped celery
60 g (2 oz) butter or margarine
½ cup (4 fl oz) tomato sauce
½ cup (4 fl oz) water
1 beef stock cube
2 tablespoons German mustard
salt and pepper
500 g (1 lb) frankfurters

Brown minced steak, onion and celery in butter in a heavy based saucepan or flameproof casserole. Add tomato sauce, water, beef stock cube and mustard, mix together thoroughly and simmer uncovered for 15-20 minutes. Season to taste with salt and pepper.
Slit frankfurters lengthways, but not quite through. Barbecue over medium coals for 7-10 minutes, turn frequently while cooking.
When heated through, serve with the meat sauce spooned over them.

Heidelberg Dinner

SERVES: 8-10
(see photograph page 1)

4 cooking apples
1 small red cabbage, coarsely shredded
½ cup (4 fl oz) apple cider
¼ cup (2 fl oz) salad oil
2 tablespoons red wine vinegar
2 tablespoons brown sugar
2 bay leaves
½ teaspoon salt
freshly ground pepper
500 g (1 lb) Polish sausages
500 g (1 lb) bratwurst sausages

Core apples, do not peel. Cut apple into thin slices. Combine all ingredients except sausages in a heavy based saucepan or flameproof casserole, mix together thoroughly. Cover and place on barbecue over medium hot coals for approximately 1 hour or until cabbage is tender, stir occasionally while cooking.
Barbecue sausages, turning frequently, cook for approximately 15-20 minutes or until sausages are evenly brown and cooked through.
Serve sausages with the red cabbage casserole.

Barbecued Polish Sausages

SERVES: 4-5

1½ cups (12 fl oz) hot water
1½ cups (12 fl oz) red wine
500 g (1 lb) Polish sausages
German mustard
8-10 slices rye bread

Pour water and red wine into a heavy based saucepan or flameproof casserole, bring to the boil. Add sausages and simmer gently for approximately 5-10 minutes.
Drain and cool sausages.
Place on barbecue and, turning frequently, cook for 15-20 minutes until evenly brown.
Serve with mustard and rye bread.

Sausages Supreme

Place thick pork sausages in a heavy based saucepan, cover with cold water and bring to the boil, simmer for 5–10 minutes. Drain and cool.
Place sausages on barbecue over medium coals, and turning frequently, cook until evenly brown.
When ready to serve sausages, slit lengthways, not quite through, and place 2–3 cold oysters inside each. Serve immediately.

Frankfurter and Pineapple Kebabs

Cut each frankfurter into 4 pieces. Alternate on skewers with pieces of canned or fresh pineapple. Brush with melted butter or margarine.
Barbecue over medium coals for 7–10 minutes or until golden brown. Turn frequently while cooking and baste with melted butter.
Toast split frankfurter rolls over coals and spread with butter.
Serve kebabs in bread rolls with mustard if desired.

Sausages with Bacon and Cheese

SERVES: 3–4

500 g (1 lb) thick pork sausages
125 g (4 oz) Cheddar cheese, sliced
6 rashers bacon, rind removed
3 tablespoons fruit chutney

Barbecue sausages over medium coals for approximately 15 minutes. Slit sausages lengthways, almost through. Place slices of cheese in the sausages and press together again. Spread bacon rashers with the chutney and wrap around the sausages, secure ends with cocktail sticks. Place on barbecue again and, turning frequently, cook until cheese begins to melt and bacon is crisp and golden brown. Remove cocktail sticks before serving.

Glazed Frankfurters

SERVES: 8–10

1 kg (2 lb) frankfurters
SAUCE:
1 cup (4 oz) canned apricots, drained and puréed
½ cup (4 fl oz) tomato sauce
⅓ cup (2 fl oz) vinegar
¼ cup (2 fl oz) sherry
2 tablespoons soy sauce
2 tablespoons honey
¼ teaspoon ground ginger
¼ teaspoon salt
freshly ground pepper

Barecue frankfurters over medium coals for approximately 7–10 minutes, turning and basting frequently with the sauce while cooking.
Serve frankfurters when hot and glazed. Heat remaining sauce in a heavy based saucepan and serve separately.
Sauce: Combine all ingredients and mix together thoroughly.

Barbecued Beef Feast, Barbecued Butterfly Lamb and Tabbouleh (see pages 23, 18 and 52).

Apricot Glazed Sausages

SERVES: 6

1 kg (2 lb) thick beef or pork sausages
Apricot barbecue sauce (see page 59)

Barbecue sausages over medium coals, turning frequently and basting with the sauce while cooking.
Barbecue sausages for approximately 15 minutes or until cooked and golden brown. Reheat remaining sauce and serve with the sausages.

Piquant Sausages

SERVES: 4

500-750 g (1-1½ lb) pork sausages
3 tablespoons tomato sauce
2 teaspoons soy sauce
1 teaspoon dry mustard
1 clove garlic, crushed
2 teaspoons white wine vinegar
1 tablespoon brown sugar

Combine the tomato sauce, soy sauce, mustard, vinegar and brown sugar in a bowl.
Make shallow slits along the length of the sausages and marinate them for 30 minutes in the mixture.
Barbecue sausages for 7-10 minutes, turning frequently, or until thoroughly cooked.

Frankfurters wrapped in Bacon

Slit frankfurters lengthways, not quite through and to within 5 mm (¼-inch) of each end. Spread inside generously with favourite pickle or relish and wrap a derinded rasher of bacon around each frankfurter, securing the ends with cocktail sticks.
Barbecue over medium coals until frankfurters are hot and bacon is crisp and brown. Remove cocktail sticks before serving.

Sausages with Plum Sauce

SERVES: 6

12 pork sausages
30 g (1 oz) butter
1 small onion, finely chopped
2/3 cup (5 fl oz) bottled plum sauce
2/3 cup (5 fl oz) water
salt and pepper
2 teaspoons Worcestershire sauce
1 teaspoon dry mustard

Melt the butter in a frying pan and sauté the onion for about 5 minutes or until soft. Add the plum sauce, water, salt and pepper, Worcestershire sauce and mustard. Simmer for 5-8 minutes until the sauce has reduced slightly. Meanwhile, prick the sausages and barbecue them for approximately 10 minutes or until thoroughly cooked.
Serve sausages with plum sauce poured over them.

Chicken Teriyaki accompanied by a mouth-watering Italian Sandwich (see pages 42 and 57).

Barbecued Poultry

Chicken can be cooked on a barbecue in a number of ways. It can be cooked whole on a rotisserie or halved or cut into portions and grilled over glowing coals. For easy eating, when catering for a large number of people, bone chickens when raw and after cooking, cut into bite size pieces and hand around on large serving plates. Chicken, cut into pieces, placed on skewers and barbecued, makes delicious kebabs, baste while cooking with your favourite sauce. When cooking chicken pieces, cook them longer on the bone side than the meat side. This protects the meat from becoming charred while cooking, it will remain moist and tender and will be golden brown when cooked. Baste the pieces of chicken before cooking with melted butter or oil and again when cooking is completed.

Barbecued Chicken Halves

SERVES: 4

4 chicken halves
MARINADE:
1 cup (8 fl oz) sherry or apple juice
½ cup (4 fl oz) salad oil
1 onion, finely chopped
1 tablespoon French mustard
1 tablespoon mixed dried herbs
1 teaspoon salt
freshly ground pepper
1 tablespoon Worcestershire sauce
1 teaspoon soy sauce

Place chicken halves in a shallow dish, pour marinade over. Cover and stand for several hours, turn meat occasionally. Drain chicken and reserve marinade. Barbecue chicken over medium hot coals for approximately 25–35 minutes or until tender. Allow more cooking time on the bone side than the flesh side. Baste with the marinade while cooking.
Marinade: Combine all ingredients and mix together thoroughly.

Barbecued Drumsticks

SERVES: 6

12 chicken drumsticks
MARINADE:
¼ cup (2 fl oz) tomato sauce
2–3 tablespoons lemon juice
2 tablespoons soy sauce
¼ cup (2 fl oz) salad oil
½ teaspoon monosodium glutamate

Place drumsticks in a shallow dish, add marinade. Cover and stand for at least 2 hours, turn drumsticks occasionally. Drain meat and reserve marinade.
Barbecue drumsticks over medium hot coals for approximately 20–25 minutes or until tender. Baste occasionally with the marinade while cooking.
Marinade: Combine all ingredients and mix together thoroughly.

Chicken on the Spit

SERVES: 4

1 x 1.5 kg (3 lb) chicken
2 teaspoons salt
freshly ground pepper
60–125 g (2–4 oz) butter or margarine, melted

Wash and dry chicken, sprinkle salt and pepper in cavity. Truss chicken firmly and insert spit rod through centre of bird from neck to tail. Make sure chicken is held firmly in place and will not work loose while cooking.
Cook over medium hot coals for approximately 1¼–1¾ hours or until tender. When cooked, drumsticks should feel soft and move easily. Baste chicken frequently with butter while cooking.
Cut chicken into 4 portions to serve.
Note: While cooking, chicken may be basted with favourite sauce or marinade instead of butter.

East Indies Barbecued Chicken

SERVES: 4

1 x 1.5 kg (3 lb) chicken
oil
salt
EAST INDIES SAUCE:
1 onion, finely chopped
1 stalk celery, finely chopped
2 tablespoons oil
2 cups (16 fl oz) chicken stock or water and chicken stock cube
½ cup stewed tomatoes
¼ apple, peeled and finely chopped
1½ tablespoons curry powder
½ teaspoon monosodium glutamate
salt and pepper

Cut chicken into 8 pieces, brush each piece with oil and sprinkle with salt. Allow chicken pieces to stand for 30 minutes. Grill chicken over glowing coals, basting frequently with East Indies Sauce and turning the pieces from time to time until tender.
To make East Indies Sauce: Sauté the onion and celery in oil until soft and golden. Add chicken stock, stewed tomatoes, apple, curry powder, monosodium glutamate and salt and pepper to taste. Simmer for 30 minutes. Serve with fresh pineapple, fruit chutney and chopped cashew nuts.

Golden Chicken

SERVES: 4

1 x 1.5 kg (3 lb) chicken
2 tablespoons curry powder
1 teaspoon salt
½ cup (5 oz) honey
2 tablespoons French mustard

Cut chicken into serving pieces. Combine
curry powder and salt and sprinkle over
chicken pieces. Mix honey and mustard
together.
Barbecue chicken over medium hot coals
for approximately 20–25 minutes or until
tender, baste frequently with the honey
mixture while cooking. Allow more cooking
time on the bone side than the flesh side.

Chicken Teriyaki

SERVES: 4
(see photograph page 38)

1 x 1.5 kg (3 lb) chicken
MARINADE:
½ cup (4 fl oz) soy sauce
¼ cup (3 oz) honey
½ teaspoon monosodium glutamate
1 clove garlic, crushed
½ teaspoon ground ginger

Cut chicken into serving pieces and place
in a shallow dish. Pour marinade over,
cover and chill for at least 8 hours, turn
meat occasionally. Drain chicken and
reserve marinade.
Barbecue chicken pieces over medium hot
coals for approximately 20–25 minutes or
until tender. Allow more cooking time on
the bone side than the flesh side. Baste with
the marinade while cooking.
Marinade: Combine all ingredients and
mix together thoroughly.

Devilled Chicken

SERVES: 4-6

2 x 1 kg (2 lb) chickens
SAUCE:
60 g (2 oz) butter or margarine
½ cup finely chopped onion
1½ cups (12 fl oz) tomato juice
⅓ cup (2 fl oz) lemon juice
1 tablespoon Worcestershire sauce
1 tablespoon paprika
1 teaspoon sugar
1 teaspoon salt
freshly ground pepper

Cut chickens into serving pieces.
Barbecue over medium hot coals for
approximately 20–25 minutes or until
chicken is tender. Allow more cooking time
on the bone side than the flesh side. Baste
with the sauce while cooking.
Serve any remaining sauce with the
chicken.
Sauce: Melt butter in a saucepan, add
onion and sauté until golden brown. Add
remaining ingredients, heat until boiling.
Keep warm while basting chicken pieces.

Barbecue the Beast

Give your friends a surprise, barbecue a lamb or sucking pig when you next entertain. What a delicious flavour, they will talk about it for months. With these recipes to guide you it is so simple.

Barbecued Lamb

For barbecuing, choose a lamb 15–17 kg (30–35) lb in weight. Allow approximately 250–375 g (½–¾ lb) carcase weight for each serving. A lamb weighing 15 kg (30 lb) will therefore serve 40–60 people. Cook lamb approximately 40 minutes for each kilo. Split lamb in half lengthways. Make small incisions in skin of lamb approximately 7.5 cm (3-inches) apart, insert slivers of garlic and fresh thyme leaves.

The larger the lamb, the further away from the coals it should be while cooking.

The lamb can be turned easily by placing each half in a stainless steel basket which hangs from a tall tripod over the barbecue or place on grill 36–41 cm (14–16 inches) above hot coals. Turn frequently and allow more cooking time on the bone side — three times longer than the skin side. While cooking, baste with a mixture of claret and finely chopped mint leaves.

When serving Barbecued Lamb at a buffet party, cut meat into bite size pieces and arrange on large trays. If guests are seated, carve meat and place on dinner plates.

Sucking Pig

For barbecuing, a sucking pig should weigh under 10 kg (20 lb). Allow approximately 500 g (1 lb) carcase weight for each serving. A pig weighing 6–7 kg (12–14 lb) will therefore serve 12–14 people. Cook approximately 40–50 minutes for each kilo.

The pig will be cooked more successfully and easily if cut in half. Cut pig lengthways down the centre and score the legs. Rub the skin with plenty of salt to give a crisp crackling.

The pig can be turned easily by placing each half in a stainless steel basket which hangs from a tall tripod over the barbecue or place on grill 36–41 cm (14–16 inches) above the hot coals. Turn frequently and allow more cooking time on the bone side — three times longer than the skin side. Too much cooking on the skin side will burn the skin and ruin the crackling.

When serving Sucking Pig at a buffet party, cut into bite size pieces and arrange on large trays. If guests are seated, carve the meat and place on dinner plates.

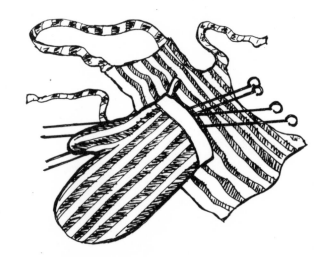

Barbecued Fish

The following recipes will appeal especially to the fishermen. Whole fish, fish steaks, fillets of fish and shellfish, all can be barbecued successfully.

Whole fish may be barbecued in wire baskets, turning frequently. No basting is required, but when cooked and ready to serve, brush the fish with butter and lemon juice and season with salt and pepper. Small fish, freshly caught, may be threaded on stainless steel skewers for barbecuing or they may be cooked in wire baskets placed flat over the fire.

Fish steaks, fillets of fish and shellfish may be barbecued directly over glowing coals or cooked in a cast iron skillet or on a hotplate. Choose which ever method you prefer. Serve the freshly barbecued fish as an appetizer or main course.

Remember fish is delicate so handle it carefully. Serve when the translucent flesh has turned opaque and flakes easily with a fork, it will be moist and tender.

Baked Stuffed Fish

SERVES: 4-6

1 x 1-1.5 kg (2-3 lb) snapper (or bass)
3 rashers bacon, rind removed
freshly ground pepper
STUFFING:
60 g (2 oz) butter or margarine
½ cup chopped onion
½ cup chopped celery
2 tablespoons finely chopped parsley
½ teaspoon salt
½ teaspoon dried thyme
1 cup (2 oz) soft white breadcrumbs

Wash fish and dry thoroughly. Place
stuffing in cavity of fish, close opening with
fine skewers or cocktail sticks. Place on
large piece of greased, doubled aluminium
foil, place bacon rashers over top and
sprinkle with pepper.
Wrap fish securely in foil and cook over
medium hot coals for approximately 1-1¼
hours or until fish flakes easily with a fork.
Turn occasionally while cooking.
Stuffing: Melt butter and place in a bowl
with remaining ingredients. Mix together
thoroughly.

Baked Trout

SERVES: 4-6
(see photograph page 2)

1 x 1-1.5 kg (2-3 lb) trout
salt and pepper
1 onion, thinly sliced
pinch of dried sage or 2 fresh leaves
pinch of thyme or 1 fresh sprig
2-3 rashers bacon

Clean the trout and place salt and pepper,
onion, sage and thyme inside cavity.
Arrange bacon rashers over the fish and
place on a large piece of greased, doubled
aluminium foil. Wrap fish securely and
cook on barbecue over medium hot coals
for approximately 1-1¼ hours or until fish
flakes easily with a fork. Turn occasionally
while cooking.
Alternatively: panfry freshly caught trout in
butter with lemon juice and finely sliced
onions or shallots for approximately 7
minutes each side, according to size and
barbecue efficiency. Top with fresh herbs
if available.

Bouillabaisse

SERVES: 6-8

1.5 kg (3 lb) fish fillets, a selection of
    bream, snapper and jewfish (or bream,
    haddock and bass)
1 small lobster
½ cup (4 fl oz) olive oil
4 carrots, thinly sliced
2 onions, thinly sliced
4 cloves garlic, crushed
2 leeks, thinly sliced
4 large tomatoes
bouquet garni (thyme, bay leaf, parsley,
    celery, rosemary)
4 large potatoes, sliced
3 cups (24 fl oz) fish stock, made from fish
    trimmings
½ teaspoon powdered saffron
salt
freshly ground pepper
24 fresh mussels in shells

Cut fish into 5 cm (2-inch) pieces. Remove
meat from lobster, cut into chunks.
Heat oil in a large heavy based saucepan
or flameproof casserole. Add carrots,
onions, garlic and leeks, sauté until golden
brown. Chop tomatoes and add to pan with
the bouquet garni.
Add pieces of fish and potato to pan, cook
for approximately 5 minutes, stir gently.
Add fish stock and seasonings and bring
to the boil. Simmer for 15 minutes. Add
mussels and crayfish meat and cook just
until mussels open.
Serve Bouillabaisse as 2 courses. The soup
followed by the fish and potatoes.

Fish Fillets with Parsley Sauce

SERVES: 6

1 teaspoon salt
freshly ground pepper
2 tablespoons salad oil
1 kg (2 lb) fish fillets, flathead (or whiting)
2 tablespoons French mustard
60 g (2 oz) butter or margarine, softened
¼ cup finely chopped parsley
¼ cup (2 fl oz) lemon juice
extra ½ teaspoon salt

Add salt and pepper to oil, rub mixture over fish fillets. Barbecue over medium coals for approximately 10–15 minutes or until fillets are lightly browned on both sides, remove from barbecue.
Combine remaining ingredients and mix together thoroughly. Spread half the mixture over fish.
Return fish to barbecue until sizzling and fish flakes easily with a fork.
Serve with remaining savoury butter.

Grilled Fish Steaks

SERVES: 4

4 fish steaks, jewfish (or halibut)
1 teaspoon salt
¼ teaspoon pepper
60 g (2 oz) butter or margarine, melted
1 tablespoon lemon juice
1 teaspoon finely chopped chervil leaves
Avocado sauce (see page 59)

Sprinkle fish with salt and pepper.
Combine melted butter, lemon juice and chervil and brush over fish.
Place fish steaks in greased wire grill and barbecue over medium coals turning once while cooking. Barbecue for approximately 10–15 minutes or until fish flakes easily with a fork. Baste with lemon butter when cooking is completed.
Serve fish with Avocado sauce.

Sole en Papillote

SERVES: 4

500 g (1 lb) fillets of sole
1 teaspoon salt
½ cup thinly sliced mushrooms
30 g (1 oz) butter or margarine
1 cup (8 fl oz) dry sherry
1 tablespoon finely chopped onion
1 tablespoon cornflour
⅓ cup (2 fl oz) cold water
2 tablespoons lemon juice
250 g (8 oz) prawns (or shrimp), shelled
1 tablespoon finely chopped parsley.

Divide fish into 4 portions and sprinkle with salt.
Sauté mushrooms in butter until tender, add sherry and onion. Blend ornflour with water until smooth, add to mushrooms and stirring continuously, bring to the boil. Simmer for 1 minute, add lemon juice.
Place each portion of sole on a piece of greased, doubled aluminium foil, cover with prawns. Turn foil up around fish and pour sauce over the top. Sprinkle with parsley and wrap fish securely.
Cook over medium hot coals for approximately 20 minutes, or until fish flakes easily with a fork.

Barbecued Lobster

SERVES: 2-4

1 large green lobster (crayfish)
125 g (4 oz) butter or margarine, melted
⅓ cup (2 fl oz) lemon juice
salt and pepper
1 clove garlic, crushed (optional)

Break lobster in half and split the tail down the centre. Combine butter, lemon juice, salt and pepper and garlic, mix together thoroughly.
Place lobster tail, shell side down, on barbecue over medium coals, baste generously with lemon butter.
Barbecue lobster for approximately 5 minutes, baste again, turn and cook for 2 minutes.
Continue to barbecue lobster in this way, 5 minutes on the shell side, 2 minutes on the meat side until lobster has been cooked for approximately 15-20 minutes in all. When lobster meat is white and the shell is bright red, the lobster is cooked, serve immediately.
Warm any remaining lemon butter and serve with the lobster.

Charcoal Grilled Prawns

SERVES: 4-6

1 kg (2 lb) green prawns (or shrimp),
    shelled and deveined
MARINADE:
1 cup (8 fl oz) olive oil
¼ cup (2 fl oz) lemon juice
½ cup finely chopped onion
2 cloves garlic, crushed
¼ cup finely chopped parsley

Place prawns in a bowl, add marinade and mix well. Cover and stand for several hours. Drain prawns.
Place in a heavy based frying pan or skillet and cook over medium coals for approximately 10-15 minutes or until cooked. Stir frequently and add a little marinade while cooking.
Serve immediately.
Marinade: Combine all ingredients and mix together thoroughly.

Seafood Kebabs

SERVES: 4-5

1 x 1 kg (2 lb) green lobster (crayfish)
250 g (8 oz) green prawns (or shrimp)
250 g (8 oz) fresh scallops
small tomatoes
large stuffed green olives
salt and pepper
60 g (2 oz) butter, melted
2 tablespoons lemon juice
2 tablespoons finely chopped parsley

Remove meat from tail of lobster, cut into chunks. Shell and devein prawns. Alternate lobster, prawns, scallops, tomatoes and olives onto skewers. Sprinkle with salt and pepper. Combine melted butter and lemon juice and brush over the kebabs.
Barbecue over medium coals for approximately 10-15 minutes, turn frequently.
Baste with lemon butter and sprinkle with parsley before serving.

Whiting with Almonds

SERVES: 4

4 whole whiting
2 tablespoons plain flour
½ teaspoon salt
freshly ground pepper
125 g (4 oz) butter or margarine, melted
60 g (2 oz) slivered almonds
¼ cup (2 fl oz) lemon juice

Wash and dry fish thoroughly. Combine flour, salt and pepper, roll fish in seasoned flour. Place fish in a greased wire grill. Barbecue over medium coals for approximately 20 minutes or until fish flakes easily with a fork, turn frequently while cooking and baste occasionally with 60 g (2 oz) butter.
Pour remaining butter in a small saucepan, heat and add almonds, stir occasionally until almonds are golden brown, add lemon juice.
Place barbecued fish on a warm serving plate and pour sauce over.
Note: Whiting may also be cooked in a heavy based frying pan or skillet over barbecue.

Herbed Grilled Fish

SERVES: 3-4

1 x 750 g (1½ lb) fish, bream (or bluefish)
fresh fennel, dill or thyme
SAUCE:
125 g (4 oz) butter, melted
1 teaspoon salt
freshly ground pepper
1 teaspoon ground coriander seed
¼ teaspoon cardamom
2 tablespoons lemon juice
1 cup (8 fl oz) yoghurt

Wash and dry fish. Brush fish inside and
out with the sauce. Place in a greased wire
grill.
Barbecue over medium coals for
approximately 30–45 minutes or until fish is
lightly brown on both sides and flakes
easily with a fork. Turn frequently and
baste occasionally with the sauce while
cooking.
Before removing fish from barbecue, place
fresh herbs on coals, the smouldering herbs
will flavour the fish.
Heat any remaining sauce and serve with
the fish.
Sauce: Combine all ingredients and mix
together thoroughly.

Vegetables, Salads and Breads

Here is a selection of accompaniments for barbecued fish, meat and poultry. Vegetables which can be cooked on the barbecue, amongst them, Ratatouille and Barbecued Baked Beans which are perfect served with barbecued chops and steaks. There are also delicious salads and hot breads to serve with your next barbecued meal.

Avocado and Grapefruit Salad

SERVES: 4

3 avocado pears, peeled, stoned and
  sliced
1 grapefruit, peeled and cut into segments
2 oranges, peeled and cut into segments
1 small lettuce
French dressing (see page 63)

Arrange prepared avocado pears,
grapefruit and oranges on crisp lettuce
leaves.
Serve French dressing separately.

Ratatouille

SERVES: 6-8

4 tablespoons olive oil
2 cloves garlic, crushed
500 g (1 lb) eggplant, thinly sliced
1 kg (2 lb) tomatoes, thinly sliced
500 g (1 lb) zucchini, thinly sliced
4 green peppers, seeded and thinly sliced
1 cup (8 fl oz) white wine or water
salt and pepper

Heat oil and garlic in a large heavy based
frying pan or skillet and brown vegetables
in turn, cooking quickly and placing them
into a deep, flameproof casserole as they
brown (add extra olive oil to pan if
necessary). When all the vegetables are
browned, pour wine over and add salt and
pepper to taste.
Simmer on barbecue for approximately 1
hour or until vegetables are tender. Do not
stir.
Serve hot as a vegetable accompaniment
or cold as an hors d'oeuvre.

Tomatoes Vinaigrette

SERVES: 6

1 kg (2 lb) firm red tomatoes
1 onion, finely chopped
2 tablespoons dried basil
½ cup finely chopped parsley
⅓ cup (2 fl oz) French dressing (see
  page 63)

Wash and slice tomatoes. Place in layers
in a salad bowl, sprinkling each layer with
onion, basil and parsley. Pour French
dressing over salad and marinate for 2
hours before serving.

Barbecued Baked Beans

SERVES: 4

30 g (1 oz) butter or margarine
125 g (4 oz) bacon pieces, chopped
¼ cup chopped celery
¼ cup chopped onion
1 x 500 g (16 oz) can baked beans
1 tablespoon horseradish relish
1 teaspoon French mustard

Melt butter in a heavy based saucepan or
fireproof casserole and add bacon, celery
and onion. Cook gently, stirring
occasionally until ingredients are golden
brown. Add remaining ingredients, stir
well, cover and cook gently on barbecue
over medium coals for approximately 20
minutes or until baked beans are hot.
Serve with barbecued frankfurters and
sausages.

Corn on the Cob

Allow 1 corn cob for each person. Select
young, tender corn cobs. Turn back husks
and strip off silk. Brush corn with melted
butter or margarine and sprinkle with salt
and freshly ground pepper. Replace the
husks and secure in 3 places with thin
florist's wire.
Barbecue corn cobs over hot coals for
approximately 15–20 minutes, or until
tender, turn frequently. When cooked,
husks will be dry and brown and corn will
be golden brown.
Serve with melted butter and salt and
pepper.
Variation: After stripping off silk, wrap a
derinded bacon rasher around each corn
cob and secure at the ends with cocktail
sticks. Replace the husks and proceed as
above.
Note: Husks may be removed from corn
cobs completely and after brushing corn
with melted butter and seasoning with salt
and pepper, wrap individually in
aluminium foil and barbecue over hot coals
for approximately 20 minutes or until
tender. Serve as above.

Coleslaw

SERVES: 6

4 cups shredded cabbage
½ cup finely chopped cucumber
½ cup finely chopped celery
¼ cup finely chopped green pepper
DRESSING:
¾ cup (6 fl oz) mayonnaise
3 tablespoons vinegar
1 teaspoon French mustard
¼ teaspoon paprika pepper
¼ teaspoon salt

Combine prepared vegetables in a salad bowl, chill. Pour dressing over and toss together gently, adjust seasoning if necessary.
Dressing: Combine all ingredients and mix together thoroughly.

French Bean Salad

SERVES: 6

750 g (1½ lb) French beans
1 small onion, finely chopped
¼ cup (1 oz) slivered almonds, toasted
French dressing (see page 63)

Top and tail beans, string and cut diagonally into 5 cm (2-inch) pieces. Cook in boiling salted water for approximately 10–15 minutes or just until tender, drain and cool. Place beans in salad bowl, add onion and just before serving, add slivered almonds and pour over French dressing. Toss together gently and serve immediately.

Tabbouleh

SERVES: 4–6
(see photograph page 37)

1 cup fine Burghul (cracked wheat)
1 cup finely chopped fresh mint
2 cups chopped parsley
½ cup finely chopped onion or shallots
1 cup (8 fl oz) lemon juice
½ cup (4 fl oz) olive or salad oil
salt and pepper
sliced tomatoes, black olives, onion rings for garnish

Rinse Burghul under warm water, drain and add half the lemon juice. Allow to soak for 1 hour. Spread mixture over a tray to dry out for approximately 2 hours. Mix in a basin the Burghul, mint, parsley, onion and remaining lemon juice and oil. Toss while seasoning with salt and pepper. Serve garnished with tomatoes, olives and onion rings and flat Lebanese bread. Ideal with carved slices of barbecued lamb or beef.

Sour Cream Potato Salad

SERVES: 8

1 kg (2 lb) potatoes, peeled
⅓ cup (2 fl oz) French dressing (see page 63)
½ cup finely chopped cucumber
½ cup finely chopped celery
¼ cup thinly sliced onion
4 hard-boiled eggs, coarsely chopped
1 cup (8 fl oz) mayonnaise
½ cup (4 fl oz) sour cream
1 tablespoon horseradish relish
salt
freshly ground pepper
2 rashers bacon, cooked and crumbled, for garnish

Cook potatoes in boiling salted water until just tender. Drain well and cut into 1 cm (½-inch) cubes. Place potato in a bowl and pour over the French dressing while potatoes are still warm. When cool, add cucumber, celery, onion and egg. Mix mayonnaise, sour cream and horseradish relish together and pour over salad. Toss together gently and season to taste with salt and pepper.
Garnish with bacon just before serving.

Caesar Salad

SERVES: 6

DRESSING:
1 clove garlic, cut
1 teaspoon salt
¾ teaspoon freshly ground black pepper
¼ teaspoon dry mustard
¼ teaspoon sugar

SALAD:
2 hearts of lettuce
2 cloves garlic, thinly sliced
¼ cup (2 fl oz) olive oil
1 cup croûtons
1 teaspoon fresh lemon juice
4 anchovy fillets
2 tablespoons tarragon vinegar
8 tablespoons olive oil
1 raw egg, unbeaten

To make dressing: Rub salad bowl with cut clove of garlic. Add salt, pepper, mustard, sugar, lemon juice and anchovy fillets, mash well until smooth. Add vinegar, oil and egg, stir well with a fork until blended.

To make Caesar Salad: Tear prepared lettuce into small pieces. Cover garlic with olive oil and leave for at least 30 minutes (overnight if possible). Use garlic flavoured oil to fry croûtons until golden on all sides. Drain on absorbent paper. Stir dressing in salad bowl. Put lettuce on top and sprinkle with parsley. Roll salad gently from bottom of bowl so that dressing coats lettuce evenly.

Sprinkle crisp croûtons and Parmesan cheese over and serve immediately.

Glazed Carrots

Select small tender carrots, scrub well. Place in boiling salted water and cook until almost tender, drain thoroughly.

Place on barbecue over hot coals and brush with melted butter or margarine and sprinkle with a little ground coriander seed. Barbecue carrots for approximately 5–7 minutes, turning frequently and basting with melted butter as they cook.

Summer Beetroot Salad

SERVES: 4

2 large beetroot, cooked
2 large potatoes, cooked
1 small cucumber
6 gherkins, sliced
1 white onion, finely chopped
1 x 500 g (16 oz) can sauerkraut, drained
French dressing (see page 63)

Peel and dice beetroot, potatoes and cucumber. Place in a salad bowl with gherkins, onion and sauerkraut.

Pour over French dressing and toss together.

Serve immediately.

Baked Potatoes

FOR EACH SERVING:

1 potato
1 tablespoon salad oil
salt and pepper

Choose firm, even sized potatoes, scrub well and dry. Prick with a fork, brush with oil and sprinkle with salt and pepper.

Wrap each potato separately in a piece of aluminium foil.

Barbecue over hot coals or directly in the coals for approximately 45 minutes–1 hour or until tender. Turn potatoes occasionally while cooking.

Serve with butter, sour cream mixed with chopped chives or cream cheese mixed with chopped parsley and salt and pepper.

Note: Onions may be cooked in the same way.

Rice Pilaf

SERVES: 4

90 g (3 oz) butter or margarine
1 cup (5 oz) long grain rice
1 clove garlic, crushed
2½-3 cups (20-24 fl oz) beef stock or water
    and 2 beef stock cubes
¼ cup (1 oz) chopped ham
2 tablespoons flaked almonds, toasted
salt and pepper

Heat butter in heavy based frying pan, add rice and garlic. Stir until rice begins to colour. Remove from heat and add stock. Cover pan and cook over medium coals for approximately 30 minutes or until rice is tender. Add additional stock if rice appears to be dry. The liquid should be absorbed by the time the rice is tender. Remove pan from heat and add ham and almonds. Stir lightly with a fork, season to taste with salt and pepper and serve immediately.
Ideal accompaniment for kebabs.

Dill, Cucumber and Grape Salad

SERVES: 4-6

1 large cucumber
2 teaspoons salt
250 g (8 oz) white seedless grapes
2 teaspoons dill seed
1 dessertspoon freshly chopped dill leaves
1 cup (8 fl oz) sour cream
freshly ground pepper

Wash and slice cucumber thinly into a bowl, leaving the peel on, sprinkle with salt. Cover and leave for 30 minutes, then drain off excess liquid. Pick washed grapes carefully off the bunch so that there are no stalks attached and mix with the cucumber. Add dill seed, chopped dill leaves, sour cream, pepper and more salt to taste if necessary.
Chill before serving.
Ideal accompaniment to barbecued poultry.

Tossed Green Salad

SERVES: 4-6

1 large lettuce
1 cucumber, peeled and thinly sliced
4 shallots, sliced
1 green pepper, seeded and sliced
French dressing (see page 63)

Wash lettuce well, drain and chill until crisp, tear into bite size pieces. Place all vegetables in salad bowl, pour over French dressing just before serving and toss salad lightly.

Grilled Mushrooms

SERVES: 4

500 g (1 lb) mushrooms
60 g (2 oz) butter or margarine
salt and pepper

Wash and trim mushrooms, slice if large. Divide into 4 portions and place each on a piece of doubled aluminium foil. Dot with butter and sprinkle lightly with salt and pepper.
Wrap mushrooms securely and barbecue over hot coals for approximately 15-20 minutes or until mushrooms are tender, turn occasionally while cooking.
Serve with barbecued steak.

Glazed Pineapple Rings

SERVES: 6-8

6-8 fresh or canned pineapple rings
GLAZE:
½ cup (6 oz) honey
1 tablespoon French mustard

Barbecue pineapple over medium hot coals for approximately 5-7 minutes or until lightly browned. Baste frequently with the glaze while cooking.
Serve with barbecued frankfurters and sausages.
Glaze: Mix honey and mustard together.

Selection of Kebabs: Prawn, Scallop and Fruit, and Steak and Pineapple (see pages 15 and 28).

Bacon Onion Rolls

SERVES: 6

6 bread rolls
60 g (2 oz) butter
2 tablespoons salad oil
2 large onions, finely chopped
6 rashers bacon, rind removed and finely chopped

Split bread rolls and butter.
Heat oil in heavy based frying pan or skillet and fry onion and bacon together until golden brown. Place mixture in rolls and wrap securely in pieces of aluminium foil. Place on barbecue over medium coals for approximately 15 minutes or until hot, turn occasionally. Serve immediately.

Italian Sandwich

(see photograph page 38)

1 loaf French bread
60 g (2 oz) butter or margarine
1 clove garlic, crushed
2 tomatoes, thinly sliced
125 g (4 oz) Cheddar cheese, thinly sliced
125 g (4 oz) corned beef or ham, thinly sliced
1 green pepper, seeded and cut into rings

Cut bread diagonally into 2.5 cm (1-inch) slices, cutting to, but not through, the bottom crust.
Cream butter with garlic, spread between slices. Place a slice of tomato, cheese, meat and green pepper between each slice of bread. Press loaf firmly together again. Wrap in aluminium foil and place on barbecue over medium coals for approximately 20–25 minutes or until cheese begins to melt and bread is hot. Turn loaf once while heating.
To serve, remove foil and cut through bottom crust of loaf.

Hot Garlic Bread

1 loaf French bread
125 g (4 oz) butter or margarine, softened
1 large clove garlic, crushed

Cut bread diagonally into 2.5 cm (1-inch) slices, cutting to, but not through, the bottom crust.
Cream butter with crushed garlic, spread between slices. Press loaf firmly together. Wrap in aluminium foil and seal securely. Heat on barbecue over medium coals for approximately 20 minutes, turn loaf once. Serve when butter has melted and bread is hot. Open foil and cut through bottom crust just before serving.
Variations: Anchovy: Omit garlic. Soak 6 anchovy fillets in milk for 30 minutes. Drain and chop finely, add to butter with 1 teaspoon anchovy sauce.
Herb cheese: Cream 2 teaspoons finely chopped parsley, ½ teaspoon finely chopped oregano leaves and 2 tablespoons grated Parmesan cheese with the garlic butter.
Herb lemon: Omit garlic. Cream 2 teaspoons lemon juice, 1 tablespoon finely chopped fresh herbs and pinch of salt with butter.
Onion: Omit garlic. Cream 2 tablespoons finely chopped onion or chives with butter.
Seeds: Omit garlic. Cream 1-2 teaspoons of celery, poppy, dill or sesame seeds with butter.

Fruit Kebabs (see page 67).

Sauces, Marinades and Relishes

Tasty piquant sauces served with barbecued meats, fish and poultry provide a variety of flavours to grilled food. Some are basted over food while it is being barbecued, others are served at the table when cooking is completed. There are marinades to tenderize and add flavour to meat. Use small heavy based saucepans when making sauces on the barbecue. Sauces for basting can be placed in fireproof pots and kept close at hand by the barbecue. These recipes will add originality to your barbecue menus.

Almond Sauce

125 g (4 oz) butter or margarine
60 g (2 oz) slivered almonds
salt
freshly ground pepper
pinch of nutmeg
2 teaspoons lemon juice
2 tablespoons finely chopped chives

Melt butter in a saucepan and add
almonds, cook gently until almonds are
golden brown. Add seasonings and lemon
juice. Before serving, add chives and mix
together thoroughly.
Serve with barbecued chicken.

Apricot Barbecue Sauce

3 tablespoons salad oil
2 tablespoons vinegar
½ cup (4 fl oz) apricot juice
½ cup (4 fl oz) tomato sauce
1 tablespoon brown sugar
2 tablespoons grated onion
½ teaspoon Worcestershire sauce
1 teaspoon salt
½ teaspoon dried oregano
dash of Tabasco sauce

Combine all ingredients together in a
saucepan and bring to the boil, stirring
occasionally. Cover and simmer gently for
10 minutes.
Baste meat with sauce during barbecuing
and serve remainder of sauce separately.
This sauce keeps well for 1–2 weeks, if
stored in a sealed container in a
refrigerator.

Avocado Sauce

1 ripe avocado pear
½ cup (4 fl oz) sour cream
1 teaspoon lemon juice
¼ teaspoon salt
freshly ground pepper
few drops Tabasco sauce

Peel avocado pear, remove stone and mash
with a fork in a mixing bowl. Add
remaining ingredients and mix together
thoroughly.
Serve with barbecued shellfish.

Barbecue Sauce

30 g (1 oz) butter or margarine
1¼ cups finely chopped onion
2 tablespoons brown sugar
1 tablespoon vinegar
1 tablespoon Worcestershire sauce
½ cup (4 fl oz) tomato sauce
¼ cup (2 fl oz) water
2 tablespoons lemon juice

Melt butter in saucepan and add finely
chopped onion, sauté until golden. Add
remaining ingredients and bring to the
boil, simmer for 15 minutes.
Serve with barbecued sausages,
frankfurters and hamburgers.

Barbecue Wine Sauce

1 small onion, finely chopped
1 clove garlic, crushed
1 cup (8 fl oz) red wine
½ cup (4 fl oz) water
½ cup (4 fl oz) olive oil
¼ cup (2 fl oz) red wine vinegar
1 teaspoon Worcestershire sauce
½ teaspoon chilli sauce
1 teaspoon sugar
2 teaspoons French mustard
1 teaspoon salt
1 teaspoon paprika pepper
¼ teaspoon Tabasco sauce

Place all ingredients in a saucepan and
bring to the boil. Simmer for 5 minutes,
strain and cool.
Use to marinate and baste meat.

Basting Sauce for Lamb

3 tablespoons olive oil
2 tablespoons white wine
½ teaspoon finely chopped fresh thyme
2 teaspoons finely chopped mint
½ teaspoon salt
freshly ground pepper

Combine all ingredients and mix together thoroughly.
Suitable for using as a marinade or basting sauce for any lamb dish.

Fiagaro Sauce

3 tablespoons tomato purée
1 tablespoon tomato paste
2 cups (16 fl oz) Hollandaise sauce (see page 60)
1 tablespoon finely chopped parsley
salt and pepper

Add tomato purée and tomato paste to Hollandaise sauce off the heat, beating constantly. Stir in parsley. Reheat gently and add salt and pepper to taste.
Serve with barbecued fish or steak.

Green Pepper Sauce

1 onion, finely chopped
2 green peppers, seeded and finely chopped
15 g (½ oz) butter or margarine
4 tablespoons water
2 tomatoes, chopped
salt and pepper
¼ teaspoon chilli sauce

Sauté onion and peppers in butter in a saucepan until golden brown. Add remaining ingredients, bring to the boil and simmer gently for 10 minutes. Adjust seasoning if necessary.
Serve hot with barbecued meats.

Hollandaise Sauce

125 g (4 oz) clarified butter
4 egg yolks
2 teaspoons lemon juice
salt and pepper

Place 30 g (1 oz) clarified butter and 4 egg yolks in the top of a double boiler. Place over hot, but not boiling water, stir quickly and constantly with a wooden spoon until butter and eggs are well combined. Slowly add remaining butter whisking the mixture constantly until sauce is well mixed and thickened. Remove top of double boiler from heat and beat sauce well for 2 minutes. Add lemon juice, salt and pepper. Place over hot water and beat for a further 2 minutes.
Note: Should the sauce curdle add 1–2 tablespoons cold water and beat well until smooth.

Mushroom Sauce

2 tablespoons chopped spring onions
2 tablespoons butter or margarine
125 g (4 oz) small mushrooms, sliced
1 teaspoon lemon juice
2 tablespoons plain flour
¼ cup (2 fl oz) dry white wine
1 cup (8 fl oz) light cream
salt
freshly ground black pepper

Sauté spring onions in melted butter in a saucepan over a medium heat for 1 minute. Add mushrooms and lemon juice and sauté until mushrooms are cooked and liquid has evaporated. Add flour and cook, stirring, for 1–2 minutes. Add wine and ¾ cup (6 fl oz) cream, and bring to the boil, stirring constantly until sauce is thick and bubbling. Remove from heat and stir in remaining cream. Add seasoning to taste, if sauce is too thick add a little more wine.
Serve with barbecued beef, veal or lamb.

Horseradish Sauce

15 g (½ oz) butter or margarine
1 tablespoon plain flour
½ cup (4 fl oz) chicken stock or water and
    chicken stock cube
2 tablespoons horseradish relish
½ cup (4 fl oz) cream
pinch of cayenne pepper
salt and pepper

Melt the butter in a saucepan, add flour
and blend together, cook for 2–3 minutes
without colouring. Add stock and, stirring
continuously, bring to the boil, simmer for
3 minutes. Add remaining ingredients and
season to taste with salt and pepper.
Serve hot with barbecued steak.

Oyster Sauce

1 bottle oysters
2 tablespoons butter or margarine
1 tablespoon plain flour
dry white wine
salt
freshly ground black pepper

Drain liquid from oysters and reserve. Cut
each oyster in half if large. Melt butter in
a saucepan over a low heat, stir in flour
until well blended, without colouring. Add
oyster liquid and bring to the boil, stirring
continuously. Add enough white wine to
give a good coating sauce consistency.
Season with salt and pepper to taste.
Serve with barbecued steak.

Redcurrant Glaze

1 cup (10 oz) redcurrant jelly
1 x 150 ml (5 fl oz) can frozen concentrated
    orange juice
1 teaspoon dry mustard
pinch of ground ginger

Combine all ingredients in a saucepan
and, stirring continuously, heat gently until
smooth.
Baste chickens with glaze while
barbecuing.

Spicy Tomato Barbecue Sauce

1 cup (8 fl oz) tomato sauce
2 tablespoons vinegar
1 tablespoon Worcestershire sauce
1 tablespoon grated onion
2 tablespoons oil or butter
1 teaspoon sugar
1 teaspoon salt
½ teaspoon garlic powder
1 teaspoon paprika
½ teaspoon allspice
½ teaspoon dry mustard

Place all ingredients together in a
saucepan and blend well until smooth.
Bring to the boil over a low heat and
simmer gently for 10 minutes.
Baste meat with sauce during barbecuing
and serve remainder of sauce separately.
This sauce keeps for 1–2 weeks if stored in
a sealed container in a refrigerator.
Serve with barbecued beef, veal, lamb,
kebabs and sausages.

Teriyaki Marinade

¾ cup (6 fl oz) canned pineapple juice
3 tablespoons soy sauce
3 tablespoons lemon juice
2 cloves garlic, crushed
1 bay leaf
pinch of ground cloves

Combine all ingredients in a screw-top jar, shake well.
Use to marinate meat immediately or store in refrigerator until ready to use.

Tomato Sauce

4 large ripe tomatoes, skinned
4 tablespoons tomato sauce
1 tablespoon red wine vinegar
2 tablespoons salad oil
2 drops Tabasco sauce
pinch of dry mustard
salt and pepper

Coarsely chop the tomatoes and mix with remaining ingredients. Season to taste with salt and pepper.
Serve with barbecued sausages and chops.

Thousand Island Sauce

1 quantity Basic Mayonnaise (see page 63)
1 hard-boiled egg, finely chopped
2 tablespoons chilli sauce
3 tablespoons finely chopped stuffed
    olives
2 tablespoons finely chopped onion
2 tablespoons finely chopped parsley
2 tablespoons whipped cream

Blend mayonnaise with egg, chilli sauce, olives, onion and parsley. Stir in cream just before serving.
Note: Substitute tomato sauce for chilli sauce if a milder flavour is preferred.

Lemon Butter

125 g (4 oz) butter or margarine
3 tablespoons lemon juice

Melt butter in a saucepan over medium heat until it foams and becomes light brown. Remove from heat and add lemon juice.
Use to baste and serve with barbecued fish and meat.

Fresh Chutney

1 apple
1 onion
3 tomatoes
3 stalks celery
1 cup pimiento
1 tablespoon finely chopped mint
1 tablespoon horseradish relish
1 clove garlic, crushed
2 tablespoons sugar
2 tablespoons vinegar
1 teaspoon salt
freshly ground pepper

Peel and grate the apple and onion. Skin the tomatoes and chop roughly. Finely chop the celery and pimiento. Place all ingredients in a saucepan and bring to the boil, simmer 4–5 minutes.
Serve hot or cold with grilled steak, chops, sausages and kebabs.

Apple and Mint Relish

1 large cooking apple
2 tablespoons apricot jam
1 tablespoon vinegar
1 tablespoon finely chopped mint
salt and pepper

Peel and grate the apple. Mix immediately with remaining ingredients in a mixing bowl, season to taste.
Serve relish with barbecued beef and lamb.

Basic Mayonnaise

2 egg yolks
½ teaspoon salt
½ teaspoon dry mustard
¼ teaspoon castor sugar
3 tablespoons fresh lemon juice (strained)
1¼ cups (10 fl oz) olive oil
1 tablespoon wine vinegar
1 tablespoon boiling water

Place egg yolks in a warm bowl. Add salt, mustard, sugar and 1 tablespoon lemon juice. Beat thoroughly. Add half oil, drop by drop, beating thoroughly all the time. When mayonnaise is as thick as stiffly whipped cream, add another tablespoon lemon juice. Still beating, add rest of oil in thin, steady stream. Stir in rest of lemon juice and wine vinegar then lastly fold in the boiling water.

Anchovy Mayonnaise

2 teaspoons anchovy sauce
1¼ cups (10 fl oz) mayonnaise (see page 63)
1 tablespoon finely chopped parsley or capers
1 tablespoon chopped dill cucumber
1 clove garlic, crushed
3 black olives, stoned and chopped
2 tablespoons cream
salt
freshly ground pepper

Combine all ingredients in a mixing bowl and mix together thoroughly, adjust seasoning if necessary.
Serve with barbecued fish.

French Dressing

3 parts salad oil
1 part vinegar
½ teaspoon salt
freshly ground pepper

Combine all ingredients together in a screw-top jar, shake well. Store in refrigerator if not being used immediately. Crushed garlic, French or English mustard or chopped herbs may be added to the basic dressing.
Olive, safflower or peanut oil may be used. There are a variety of vinegars to choose from, cider, red wine, white wine and various vinegars flavoured with herbs.

Satay Sauce

1 onion, finely chopped
2 cloves garlic, crushed
2 tablespoons salad oil
1 cup (8 fl oz) dry white wine
¼ cup (2 fl oz) dry sherry
¼ cup (2 fl oz) soy sauce
2 tablespoons tomato purée
1 tablespoon peanut butter

Sauté onion and garlic in oil in a saucepan until golden.
Add wine, sherry, soy sauce and tomato purée. Bring to the boil and simmer until reduced by a third. Add peanut butter and mix thoroughly.
Use sauce to baste and serve with satays.

Apple Sauce

3 green cooking apples
¼ cup (2 fl oz) water
1 teaspoon butter or margarine
sugar to taste
lemon juice to taste

Peel and core apples, slice into a saucepan
and add water. Cover and simmer gently
until soft enough to mash to smooth pulp.
If Apple Sauce contains too much liquid,
reduce until the right consistency is
obtained. Stir butter into warm sauce. Add
sugar and lemon juice.
Serve with barbecued pork.

Peanut Sauce

1 onion, finely chopped
1 clove garlic, crushed
60 g (2 oz) butter or margarine, melted
1 tablespoon soy sauce
3 tablespoons peanut butter
1 tablespoon lemon juice
½ cup (4 fl oz) cream

Sauté onion and garlic in butter in a
saucepan until golden. Add soy sauce,
peanut butter and lemon juice and mix
together thoroughly, cool. Before serving,
add the cream.
Delicious served with barbecued steaks
and chops.

Desserts and Drinks

What a delicious idea, barbecued desserts. Here are recipes for your next barbecue, everyone will love them. Children can make their own Fruit Kebabs while adults eat Fruit Flambés, a wonderful finale to a meal eaten out of doors.

Make a large jug of ice cold Cider Cup or Sangria when the weather is hot or try Mulled Wine in the cooler months, your party will be off to a swinging start.

Peaches Italienne

SERVES: 6

12 canned peach halves, drained
6 tablespoons sherry
⅓ cup (1½ oz) slivered almonds, toasted
ice cream or whipped cream for serving

Place 2 peach halves on each piece of aluminium foil. Turn sides of foil up and pour 1 tablespoon of sherry over each serving.
Seal foil firmly and place on barbecue over hot coals for approximately 10 minutes or until peaches are warm.
To serve, remove peaches from foil packages, sprinkle with slivered almonds and serve with ice cream or whipped cream.

Pineapple Fruit Salad

SERVES: 6-8

1 large ripe pineapple
4 bananas
juice of ½ lemon
2 tablespoons fresh orange juice
4 oranges
pinch of salt
1 red skinned apple, unpeeled and diced
1 pear, peeled and diced
1½ cups seedless small green grapes
pulp of 4 passionfruit
2-3 tablespoons icing sugar, sifted
250 ml (8 fl oz) cream and castor sugar for serving

Slice base and top from pineapple to form a lid. With a long, thin bladed knife remove outer skin from flesh keeping skin intact. Remove cylinder of pineapple flesh. Wrap and chill skin. Remove core from pineapple and cut flesh into 2.5 cm (1 in) chunks. Peel bananas, slice diagonally and drench with lemon juice. Secure base of pineapple to skin of pineapple with cocktail sticks. Arrange pineapple shell on platter lined with banana or orange leaves. Combine half pineapple with drained bananas and orange juice. Peel oranges, remove pith and cut into segments. Add salt, apple, pear, grapes and passionfruit pulp. Chill for 30 minutes. Sprinkle with icing sugar, spoon fruit into pineapple shell. Top with lid.
Serve with whipped cream.

Fruit Punch

SERVES: 14-16

1 cup (7 oz) sugar
1 cup (8 fl oz) water
2 cups (16 fl oz) canned pineapple juice
1 cup (8 fl oz) orange juice
juice of 1 lemon
5 cups (1.25 litres) cold weak tea
2½ cups (20 fl oz) ginger ale
2 passionfruit
sprigs of mint
6 strawberries, chopped
crushed ice

Place sugar and water in a saucepan over gentle heat. Stir until sugar is dissolved, boil for 2-3 minutes. Cool and add fruit juices and tea. Chill well and just before serving add cold ginger ale, passionfruit pulp, sprigs of mint, strawberries and crushed ice.
Serve in chilled glasses.

Sangria

SERVES: 6-8

2½ cups (20 fl oz) red wine, claret or Burgundy
2 tablespoons brandy
1 tablespoon gin
4 lumps sugar
juice of 2 oranges
juice of 1 lemon
2 cups (16 fl oz) soda water
ice cubes
thin slices or orange and lemon for garnish

Place all ingredients except soda water, ice cubes and sliced fruit in a large jug. Mix thoroughly and place in refrigerator to chill, stir occasionally.
When ready to serve, add soda water, ice cubes and sliced fruit.

Mulled Wine

SERVES: 4

2½ cups (20 fl oz) red wine, claret or
  Burgundy
juice of ½ lemon
3 cloves
2 tablespoons castor sugar
stick of cinnamon

Place all ingredients in a saucepan. Bring
to the boil and simmer for 2–3 minutes,
stirring continuously.
Strain and serve.

Cider Cup

SERVES: 6–8

ice cubes
grated rind of 1 lemon
5 cups (1.25 litres) cider
1 tablespoon maraschino
1 tablespoon curacao
1 tablespoon brandy
3 cups (24 fl oz) soda water

Place ice cubes and grated lemon rind in
a large jug. Add remaining ingredients,
mix well and serve immediately.

Fruit Kebabs

Select a variety of fruits in season and cut
into thick slices or chunks. Try whole
strawberries, large grapes, kiwi fruit,
chunks of banana, pineapple or melon,
sliced apple or peaches, and thread onto
a skewer. Just prior to cooking brush with
melted butter, sprinkle over with sugar and
cook quickly over hot coals until just glazed
and warm. Do not overcook. Serve
immediately.

Baked Apples

SERVES: 6

6 cooking apples
½ cup (3 oz) brown sugar
¼ cup (1 oz) chopped walnuts
¼ cup (1 oz) chopped raisins
1 teaspoon ground cinnamon
30 g (1 oz) butter or margarine
whipped cream for serving

Core apples and score skin around the
middle. Combine sugar, walnuts, raisins
and cinnamon in a mixing bowl, mix
together thoroughly. Place each apple on
a piece of doubled aluminium foil, stuff with
the mixture and dot with butter.
Wrap securely in foil and place on
barbecue over medium hot coals for
approximately 30–45 minutes or until
tender. Turn once while cooking.
Serve with whipped cream.

Fruit Flambés

Pineapple, peaches and strawberries are
all ideal.
Insert stainless steel skewers through
whole pineapple and place on barbecue
over hot coals and when warmed through,
remove skin and cut into chunks. Place fruit
on a metal tray, heavy based frying pan
or skillet, sprinkle with brown sugar and
rum. Warm over fire again, ignite and
serve flaming.
Peel, halve and stone fresh freestone
peaches, fill cavity with brown sugar and
rum or brandy. Place on barbecue over hot
coals until warmed through. Place on a
metal tray, heavy based frying pan or
skillet, pour over more rum or brandy and
ignite. Serve flaming.
Place strawberries on a metal tray, heavy
based frying pan or skillet, sprinkle with
brown sugar and rum or brandy, heat over
barbecue, ignite and serve flaming.
Note: At buffet parties, place cocktail sticks
in piece of fruit before serving.

Banana Delight

FOR EACH SERVING:

1 banana
4 marshmallows
30 g (1 oz) dark cooking chocolate,
  chopped

Peel banana and cut in half lengthways.
Cut marshmallows in halves with scissors.
Place banana on a piece of aluminium foil,
cover with marshmallows and chocolate.
Seal foil firmly and place on barbecue over
hot coals for 10–15 minutes, or until banana
is tender and marshmallows and chocolate
melt.
Serve in foil packages.
Note: This sweet is ideal for children's
barbecue parties.

Hawaiian Oranges

FOR EACH SERVING:

1 orange
1 tablespoon brown sugar
pinch of cinnamon
1 tablespoon rum
7.5 g (¼ oz) butter or margarine
whipped cream or ice cream for serving

Peel orange and separate into segments.
Place on a piece of aluminium foil. Turn
sides of foil up, sprinkle with sugar,
cinnamon and rum and dot with butter.
Wrap securely in foil and place on
barbecue over hot coals for approximately
15 minutes. Turn once while cooking.
Serve with whipped cream or ice cream.

Terms used in the Barbecue Cookbook

Baste: To moisten food while cooking with fat, oil or a special sauce or marinade to prevent drying and to add flavour.

Chilli Sauce: A hot pepper sauce, not to be confused with the milder chilli sauce.

Cornflour: Cornstarch.

Grill: To broil — to cook by direct heat over hot coals.

Marinate: To stand food in a liquid for a certain length of time to add flavour, or, as in the case of some meats, to tenderize.

Minced Steak: Ground beef.

Sear: To brown outer surface of meat very quickly by intense heat. It improves the appearance of the meat and keeps the flavour and meat juices inside.

Score: To cut narrow grooves or gashes part way through the outer surface of food.

Shallot: Spring onion.

Truss: To tie chicken with string or strong thread laced around metal skewers to hold its shape while cooking.

Index